The A to Z of Time Management

The A to Z of Time Management

Lynne Wenig

ALLEN & UNWIN

To my family, friends, colleagues and workshop participants who have shared their successes and their failures and who, as well as the author, are still trying to find out where the time goes and why it goes where it goes.

© Lynne Wenig 1993

First published in 1993 by
Allen & Unwin Pty Ltd
9 Atchison Street, St Leonards, NSW 2065 Australia

National Library of Australia
Cataloguing-in-Publication entry:

Wenig, Lynne, 1937– .
The A to Z of time management.

Bibliography.
ISBN 1 86373 506 2.

1. Time management. I. Title.

650.1

Set in 10½/11½ Baskerville by DOCUPRO, Sydney
Printed by Australia Print Group, Maryborough, Victoria

10 9 8 7 6 5 4 3 2 1

Contents

CONTENTS

THE A TO Z OF TIME MANAGEMENT

CONTENTS

CONTENTS

Figures

How to use this book

This is a book of time-saving ideas. It is different from other books on the topic because it does not propose the one right answer to your time pressures and frustration. *There is no one right answer!* There are usually numerous approaches to dealing with any time management hurdle.

It is up to you to choose—and use—those ideas which might work for you. To help you make your choices, there are three ways you can approach this book:

- Read it from cover to cover, noting those ideas which will create value for you, and looking for new perspectives on some old problems.
- Look through the Contents page, find an A, B or a Z of interest and read about it.
- Utilise the 'Quick reference guide' at the end of the book. This is organised according to topic and enables you to focus at a glance on a bunch of ideas that relate to that topic.

Once you have identified a strategy that you would like to attempt, start putting it into practice immediately. You may experience some disappointments. Don't despair. Try to be patient and keep up your commitment as you gradually try a new technique or change an old habit.

Your mind is the ultimate organising tool. I hope that using it, together with this book, will help save you time.

A

Accelerated learning

An integrated system of learning, also known as Suggestopedia. Using accelerated learning enables you to retain and recall materials, learn a new skill or break a bad habit in a shorter than normal time. It combines a variety of techniques that Dr Moni Lai Storz in *Mind–Body Power* says are based on the beliefs that the conscious and paraconscious minds work together as a team, that 'suggestion is the means to tap the stored reserves of the human being', and that people will find it easiest to learn if they 'do it under conditions of pleasure, joy and relaxation'. To accelerate your learning:

1 Write an **affirmation** stating what you want to achieve— your goal.
2 Do ten minutes of physical exercise to increase your heart rate.
3 Put on some largo rhythm music (any Baroque music will do), or music specifically prepared for accelerated learning.
4 Do deep rhythmic breathing until very relaxed.
5 Mentally state your affirmation to yourself.
6 Creatively visualise yourself achieving your goal.

Repeat this process daily until you have 'accelerated' to where you want to go.

Accessories

Serviceable objects of which people have too few or too many. Accessories for paperwork include stationery holders, magazine files, stacking drawers, and systems that hang on walls. Telephone accessories include headsets, answering machines, card files and clocks. For the computer there are anti-glare filters, sound covers, diskette boxes, keyboard extenders and tilt stands. Clear or translucent accessories increase visibility. Meander through a large office-supplies store and purchase the latest. A word of caution. Each time you add a new item, define its purpose and make a habit of using it. When it has outlived its value, get rid of it.

Accountability

Specific results to be achieved. Accountability forms a means of assessing performance; it is a way of getting feedback which tells whether work has been done.

To make someone accountable means monitoring tasks and confronting the team member when mistakes have been made, the task is not on schedule or the work has not been satisfactory. This is not easy. Most managers prefer to ignore the situation—or focus on the next task—thus preventing the team member from learning from mistakes. It also allows managers to complain to their peers about the poor quality of staff that the personnel department keeps hiring.

Action

Something you usually take when faced with a problem. Before you act, stop and define what the problem is. Then there are four ways you can go:

1 *Block.* Take immediate action and remove the cause of the problem.
2 *Deflect.* If you do not know the cause of the problem, act to prevent things becoming worse.
3 *Change.* Alter the situation which may have caused the problem.
4 *Hold.* If plan A fails, have a contingency plan to keep things on hold or move to plan B.

Activity trap

When motion and exertion take on a meaning by themselves. Organisations are full of people who walk rapidly down corridors clutching files and looking frantic. When you are caught in the activity trap you have lost sight of the purpose of your task, and the activity itself has become important. It usually is an indication of the absence of clear objectives.

Addictivities

Things we substitute for what must be done; habitual responses to stress. For example, if you're stalling on writing a report that you are nervous, anxious or depressed about, you will smoke, overeat, sleep, ride the exercise bike, play solitaire— anything but write the report. Some of us are expert at substituting 'busy-ness' for actual work.

How to change this pattern? Note down your addictivities. Find out the answers to the who, what, when, where and why questions. *Who* are you working with (or around) when you revert to an addictivity? *What* are they distracting you from? *When* are you most commonly diverted? *Where* are you usually when it happens? *Why* do you think it happens?

Once you have the answers to these questions, you need to devise your strategy for change. As soon as you catch yourself engaging in an addictivity, start talking to yourself. Say your 'stopper'—a word or phrase which reminds you about your behaviour, then give yourself 5 to 15 minutes before you act. It usually works.

Adrenalin addiction

One of the most unhealthy work habits. As you create pressure and crisis for yourself, you get a feeling of importance, excitement and challenge. This causes the hormone adrenalin to surge into your system. As this happens you get various symptoms such as a pounding heart, rapid breath, and an increase in blood pressure. This is OK when you are running a marathon, but when you experience the same changes during a work crisis it's trouble. What's more, sitting at your workstation or desk means there is no chance to get rid of the excess. The result? High blood pressure, ulcers and other stress symptoms.

Affirmations

General or *specific* statements about one's self that are intended to help formalise a personal goal. Affirmations come in many patterns. They can be written down, said loudly, whispered, expressed silently, even chanted. Because they are so simple, their impact is frequently misunderstood. When combined with visualising they become a particularly powerful way of changing behaviour. It helps if you:

1 Make a short, simple, clear statement.
2 State your affirmation positively and in the present tense as if it already exists.
3 Affirm what you want, not what you don't want—such as 'I am finishing my reports on time', not 'I don't want to be late with my reports'.
4 Choose affirmations that feel right to you.

If you choose to write down your affirmations, use a separate card or piece of paper for each. Read it aloud three times a day for at least 21 days.

Agenda

The alleged plan for the way a meeting is to proceed. The use of the word 'alleged' as part of the definition is deliberate as anyone who has ever attended a meeting knows. To help speed your meeting time:

1 Make your agenda clear and to the point.
2 Attach a time (start and finish) to each item.
3 Put the most important items *first*—before the minutes of the previous meeting.
4 Attach a name (or initials) for action to each item.
5 Specify any pre-reading or special preparation needed.
6 Allow a five minute limit for a status or results check on previously assigned projects.
7 Distribute the agenda at least one week before the meeting.
8 Use the speedy notice/agenda/minutes/action-list/names combo (see figure 1).
9 Keep the agenda in mind at all times.

4

Figure 1   T-form agenda

PLANNING COMMITTEE MEETING

Date: 12 September 1993

Time: 10:30 am

Place: Meeting Room A

AGENDA ITEM	NOTES (minutes)
10:15 Summary of key budget changes (Harry)	Suggested changes were approved as per circulated notes.
10:45 Nominations for new member of budget group (Chair to handle)	Jocelyn Brown — new member
10:55 Site visits (Jane L.)	3 visits arranged.
11:10 (etc.)	

Alternatives principle

An assumption that there are always alternative ways to do a task. Following the alternatives principle allows you to break out of boring time trap routines. It means that you are always looking for ways to combine ideas, to shorten the time it takes to do something, to create a new procedure.

Answering machine

A thing that goes bip, blink, wink in the night. Well, not just the night but the day also. Also known as answerphones, we either love 'em or hate 'em. One thing is certain, and that is that they're here to stay.

There are many uses for answering machines. They allow you to receive calls and hear messages which were recorded when you were not at home. They allow you to screen your calls. A memo facility allows you to record a reminder note to be replayed when you check for messages. With a remote unit or a special beeper you can retrieve messages when you are away from the office or from home.

Some machines have an inbuilt talking clock which advises day and time of calls and a visual display showing number of messages recorded. Answering machines are much more in vogue now in large organisations where they are turned on when a staff meeting is in progress, or when everyone in a department decides to lunch together for a change—and why not?

To avoid garbled messages from hotel staff, take a minia-ture machine with you when you travel and install it in your room.

Want to remember to do something later? Ring and leave yourself a message! Racing for a meeting? Turn the machine on 15 minutes before you are ready to leave to avoid last minute interruptions. Trying to finish a project without inter-ruptions? Turn on the answering machine. Use your machine to screen calls and decide whether to respond.

Think carefully about your recorded message. Some people seem to think that because they are speaking into a micro-phone they need to speak more slowly. Nonsense. We hear at exactly the same rate whether we're listening to a machine or to a person. There are some good arguments for speaking even more quickly than normal—as long as your voice is clear. Be as creative with your message as you wish, but remember that its 'tone' should reflect your personality and your busi-ness. Update the message regularly. Add a seasonal greeting if appropriate. And for those of you who work from home, please don't tell potential burglars that you are *out* for a few hours. 'Not available right now' is all they need to know.

Ants

Low-payoff tasks and activities you need to learn to stop doing.

People who are restless and impatient have a habit of working on their *ants* instead of their A-1 priority.

Spend more time on planning and setting priorities. Try grouping *ants* of the same species and dealing with them at a special *ant*-time of the day, otherwise they will continue to march into your office in an endless file. Find a *symbolic* form of talcum powder or ant killer to stop or delay your *ants*.

Appointments

The most important appointments are the ones we make with ourselves. We tend to think that our **diary** or appointment book is there only to make dates with other people. It's not. This book is a most important planning and scheduling tool.

Some basic hints for managing appointments with other people:

1 Know the exact purpose of the appointment so that you are fully prepared. Asking the right questions at the time the appointment is established will help.
2 If your assistant or a colleague has made the appointment for you, Point 1 above still applies.
3 Allow at least 15 minutes between appointments to catch your breath, but group them carefully so that you don't end up travelling back and forth across the city—or up and down in the lift—two or three times.
4 If someone is likely to cancel, always have a contingency plan.
5 Take some reading material in your **briefcase** in case of waiting time.
6 *Always* confirm your appointments on the day, or in the late afternoon prior to the appointment day.

ASAP

One of the most useless acronyms in time management. What is *your* first reaction when someone asks you to do something 'as soon as possible'? Exactly. If it's a file you drop it on the nearest pile or throw it casually into your in-tray. If it's the result of a face-to-face discussion you *may* make a note of it in your diary.

If you really want something done, request it by a specific date and time. If your request is in writing, put a note on the paper asking to 'have this on my desk by 10 am Friday, 3/6'. If in conversation say, 'I need this by 3 pm Thursday, 12 July. Is that a problem for you?'. If it is a problem, negotiate an agreed date but NEVER, NEVER, NEVER yield to the temptation of the ineffective, unproductive, worthless ASAP.

Authority

Whatever influence a person possesses that enables something to get done. It is the right to act, to make decisions, and to tell another person to do something. If you are worried about how to transfer the initiative in a delegated task to a team member, try delegating authority. This is the foundation which allows them to fulfil their responsibility.

Authority can be derived from a title, from holding a specific position, from privilege, experience, knowledge or resources. Some people have 'natural' authority which derives from their personality and ability to work well with others.

Managers need to be clear about the extent of authority being delegated and to match it with the skill level of the individual. Never *assume* someone knows how much authority they have. Make it explicit and sufficient.

Availability hours

These are times when you are available to members of your team or others without an appointment. It is one way of controlling the open door. Create special availability hours for yourself. Use signs posted prominently to tell people about your hours. If you don't let your team know your availability hours, you are less likely to make yourself available, thus getting a reputation for having a 'closed door'.

B

Back talk

In a healthy environment, this is a free flow of information which creates and maintains good communication. If you run a tight, 'need to know' or 'need to be right' ship, then you won't experience much back talk. Plenty of back talk leads to high quality new ideas, better two-directional feedback and increased **productivity**.

Backing off

A positive decision to delay or stop. Rather than persevering when your energy is low and the ideas won't flow, stop—and back off. Backing off is very different from procrastinating, which occurs when you haven't even started.

When you do decide to back off, make some plans which will make it easier for you to start again. Finish the page you are writing, or make one more call to finish the sequence. Leave yourself a written note to remind you of where you might go next. If you stopped because you were stalled, try to note down the reason why you were blocked.

Once you resume your task after a back off, your work will be more prolific and enjoyable.

Backwards planning

A simple system for **planning** the time required to finish a project. Start by listing all the steps required, working backwards from the deadline. Estimate the time required for each step. Then allocate mini-deadlines for each of the steps, still working backwards.

Mark McCormack in *Success Secrets* describes how important it is to plan backwards to keep moving forward.

> Like most people, I have a fairly predictable morning routine, made up of necessary tasks and pleasant rewards. I know, for example, that I need thirty minutes to get dressed and ten minutes to get to the office, but I also want fifteen minutes for exercises, twenty minutes to read the paper, ten minutes to read overnight faxes, thirty minutes for dictation, and five minutes to think about that eight o'clock meeting.
>
> That's two hours of time which, working backwards, tells me I have to wake up no later than six o'clock. To get a later start means I sacrifice something, ususally one or more of my rewards. That kind of loss is no way to start the day.

Bartering

Exchanging a service for a service (or goods). This makes for sensible time management. Everyone has something that someone else needs. If you have a job that you need to do and don't want to do it—or don't have the best set of skills to do it—why not barter?

Behaviour change

Changes in action and conduct. Changing time management habits means changing behaviour. As some actions are semi-automatic, you also need to increase your level of awareness about your conduct. To change behaviour you need to:

1 Want to change.
2 Understand what needs to be changed and know, or find out, how to go about doing it. This means doing some time and self analysis.
3 Devise a good, well thought out plan for change.
4 Carry out your plan.
5 Practise creative **visualisation** to help reinforce the behaviour change and to see yourself doing things in the new way.

Bill paying

Something from which there is no escape. Everyone experiences the pain that comes at bill-paying time. A sensible bill management system takes away the edge and helps relieve the suffering.

Buy yourself a file or folder in which to sort your bills. A cardboard concertina file or a looseleaf folder with plastic pockets will do nicely. Divide whatever device you use into sections. Have sections based on the type of bills you receive, e.g. medical, credit card, insurance, dental, car, household. Have a section for 'unpaid bills' also. You may wish to expand your bill-paying system into a financial management system, in which case you can have sections for bank statements, real estate, investment details and tax.

When a bill arrives, check that it's yours. If it is, highlight the due date and file it in your 'unpaid bills' section. You might like to consider filing bills in order of receipt so that you pay that way, or you may have other priorities.

Once every two weeks, take out your file, check your bills and pay them. Once a month is risky for bill paying as it's easy to miss a due date. More frequently than once a fortnight gets to be tedious. Try to pay your bills in the same place, at the same time, using the same routine. This is a basic time management habit-forming rule. As you work through your bills, devise a system for sorting out those items which will be needed for tax purposes. You can do this by using a coloured pen or self-adhesive dots, or by putting those bills into a special tax section. This can save you and/or your accountant some trouble when it's *that* time again. Once the bills are paid, file them under the sections you've marked. When the financial year turns, get another folder and start again.

Billable time

The most basic (and most common) form of fee arrangement. If your job involves working directly for clients, the time basis on which you charge is known as billable time. One of the pluses of billable time is that the client assumes the risk. And since the project may require more time than initially perceived, the client could face a substantial bill. Details of time spent, therefore, need to be carefully recorded.

You can purchase pre-printed billable time forms although most large organisations have their own forms. To help keep track of your hours:

1   Unless you're one of the lucky people who have an 'in-built' clock, obtain a beeping device or a digital watch which has been set to go off at regular intervals. When you hear the bip, note down the time and what you are doing on your prepared form.

2   Carry a bunch of small pieces of paper, index cards or a pad in your purse or pocket. Each time you begin a new task, write the task and the time on the paper and put it in a special box. You might like to use brightly coloured pads for this to distinguish these notes from any other and to help remind the right side of your brain to use them. Every day or so, write up your time sheets from these slips of paper or alternatively pass over the box of papers and delegate this chore.

3   Obtain a small dictating machine. Record your start and stop times and the task into your machine and pass the tape along for someone else to transcribe to your time sheets. Don't forget that **travel time**, telephone calls, writing, keying of notes and computing time may all be considered billable time.

Bio-rhythms

Orderly physiological fluctuations or cycles which continually influence when we wake, how we sleep, when we love, and how effectively we work or play. Cyclical variations in physical and emotional behaviour were first recorded in the 1880s. Later studies showed intellectual variations as well.

Bio-rhythms are caused by an inner clock which influences our body temperature and metabolic rate. This 'clock' is driven by electrical impulses in the brain, which vibrate at about 10 cycles per second. The impulses are unique to each individual.

The emotional bio-rhythm cycle is 28 days. During the first 14 days we are 'up', positive, creative and have a high **motiv-**

ation to succeed. During the 14 days of the downswing we get a bit short-tempered. The physical cycle is 23 days. During the first 11.5 days we have tremendous **energy**, can work for long periods without tiring and are better coordinated. During the second 11.5 days we tire more easily and our courage, will power and physical drive are limited. The intellectual cycle is 33 days with the upswing period lasting 16.5 days. During this period we have enhanced powers of reasoning, judgment, memory and learning. After 16.5 days it is all downhill. The most 'critical' days during these cycles are those days in which the rhythm changes either up or down. The existence of rhythms in the body is now very well documented.

In addition to these cycles, we each have a personal daily rhythm of energy highs and lows. Some of us are 'fowls' with our peak in the morning. Others are 'owls' with energy peaks in the evening. There are even a few people who peak around midday. It has been suggested that people have five different mental energy capability levels during the day: *peak level* when you are at your best, *good level* when you're better than average but not at your best, *average level* when you can carry out complex activities if you aren't trying to learn them, *relaxed, pleasant level* when you can function if you stay with the easy things and *low level* when you don't want to think or make decisions.

If you are looking to improve your time management and your performance, it would be valuable to identify your basic patterns and energy levels. Start by listing in a notebook your activities covering a variety of tasks. Alongside each activity you've listed, note the level of energy you think you need to perform the task well. Then take a log of your energy during a week, noting what you are doing, when you are doing it and what your energy level is actually like. Comparing your list with your log will give you a wealth of information with which to better plan and manage your time.

Begin by scheduling your high priority, high payoff tasks into your high energy or prime time. Schedule routine tasks and appointments into your low energy periods.

Blocking in

Allocating time on a daily, weekly or monthly schedule for a particular purpose. Blocks are usually made for high priority or special tasks. Time can be blocked in *horizontally*, using the same time each day, or *vertically*, say for Thursday morning.

If finding chunks of concentrated working time is a problem for you, start small—say just 15 minutes a day. Once this becomes routine, you can begin to lengthen the time of your blocking in.

Blocks

Things which inhibit our ability to make a decision. The most common blocks are:

1 *Habit.* We repeat worn-out routine, go to the same places and see the same people because this is the easiest, most comfortable way.
2 *Fatigue.* We are too tired, overwhelmed with work, and there is no end in sight.
3 *Voluntary direction change.* We start doing something half-heartedly because we believe that we can always change it if it doesn't work out.
4 *Fears.* We worry about what will happen if we get a task wrong or make a mistake. What if we run out of time? Who will know about it? Each of these fears, or any combination, goes through our mind and blocks us from doing what really needs to be done.

Boss

One of the biggest causes of wasted time. Don't fritter away your valuable time trying to talk the boss into changing. Clarify (in writing is better) any inconsistencies in **delegation** and request specific due dates on all assignments. If **deadlines** change, inform your boss. If you need to propose alternative times, think of a *very short* presentation with which to make your case. Remember! The fewer decisions the boss has to make the better.

If desperate measures are called for, do a **time log** for yourself over a couple of weeks. If the boss is really the problem the log will show it. Present the data when the boss appears to be in a receptive frame of mind. Say something like, 'I have been concerned lately about how to make the best use of my time. May I show you the results of my time log so that we can discuss them?'. Exercise caution. As the expression goes, 'softly, softly catchee monkey'.

Of course, if you have been completely honest when filling in your time log, it may be revealed that the boss isn't the problem after all.

Bouncer

Someone who is easily diverted, bounces from task to task, and goes off in several directions at the same time. This very rubbery behavioural style is exceptionally common. Bouncers sometimes ricochet because they need variety and excitement. This is a particular concern with the right-brain dominant (see **Brain dominance**). They get bored with the same assignment and need constant variety. Bouncers also leap up frequently because it makes them feel busy or because they are frustrated with something they are doing and want a distraction.

Bouncers don't stick to **priorities** or **deadlines**. This leaves their team mates floundering, confused and anxious about deadlines. Bouncers do have some positive features. They can be stimulating to work with as they are forever coming up with new ideas. Given variety, they are also good at keeping themselves (and you) motivated.

If you have a tendency to bounce, make sure you have a good time manager working on your team, preferably someone with a forceful personality who will push for project completion. When a job needs to be finished, remove all distractions—phone off hook, door closed—clear your desk of everything except what you are working on. Use your high **energy** time for high priority tasks and strive for mini goals.

Brain dominance

The side of the brain which you 'prefer' to use. Psychologists and other scientists have conducted a number of experiments which have shown that each of the two sides or hemispheres of the brain has its own way of doing things. The left brain (hemisphere) also controls the right side of the body, and the right brain the left side of the body.

The left brain is used for speaking, reading, writing and analysing. It is the logical, rational, serious, idea-linking and reasoning side. The right brain is irrational and illogical. It is used for holistic thinking, recognising similarities, insight, visualising and spatial perceptions. It deals with spontaneity, feelings, intuition and our sense of humour.

Almost everyone has a preferred or dominant side and uses that side more often than the other. Right-brain dominant people like trying new things, and prefer excitement and change in their lives. The more unpredictable something is, the happier the right brain. Left-brain dominant people prefer logic and order. Happiness for them is predictability.

The best time managers are those who most frequently integrate the two sides of the brain and get them working together. Your right brain might think up a new and creative solution to a problem, but your left brain will have to tell you how much it will cost and whether the idea is feasible or not.

Goal setting, **planning**, prioritising, putting things in writing and using time management diaries and **'to do' lists** is easy for left-brain dominant people. Of course, if they are working on the wrong project, or using ideas which are outmoded and ineffective, then all that organising is largely wasted. Because of this the left-brain time manager needs to be constantly exploring new ways of doing things.

Right-brain time managers never seem to have time to plan, and the very thought of it is often abhorrent to them. They constantly need to find new tools to help them remember to write things down. Bright coloured 'to do' pads in interesting shapes—perhaps a different one for each day of the week—can help. They need to be prompted to keep a diary and to keep it up to date, and reminded that time *is* money. Both left- and right-brain dominant people would be wise to team up with someone whose brain preference is their opposite. This means that they will jointly be able to gain the highest productivity and results.

Brainstorming

A way of drawing on individual creativity. It is one of the oldest

16

forms of systematic group problem solving. Try it with your team, looking for ways to improve the group's time management.

Brainstorming works best with a group of 6–12 people in sessions of about an hour, although less time is often sufficient. A moderator takes charge, a problem is stated, solutions are asked for and a recorder notes them down. The group is encouraged to spontaneously create as many ideas as possible with no critical remarks allowed. 'Freewheeling' (the wilder the ideas the better) and 'hitchhiking' (combining and improving) are encouraged. Quantity is wanted. Once ideas have been generated, they are screened and evaluated.

This technique draws on both sides of the brain. The right brain works to generate the ideas, while the left brain is used for the evaluation.

Briefcase

A trademark (and sometimes a status symbol) used by busy people which forms a link between the office and home. It can be decorative, a storage device, or a functional and practical time management aid. It is a *brief*case, not a suitcase, and should be used accordingly.

Hand-me-down briefcases are out. Buy one specifically for *your* needs. Select carefully as they come in all shapes and sizes with a variety of pockets, flaps and slots (both inside and outside).

Plan the way you will organise your briefcase. Keep duplicates of your basic tools (pens, paper, paper clips, etc.) in it to avoid excessive transfer of materials from desk to briefcase and back again. If you do a large amount of travelling, you may wish to have a separate briefcase for this purpose. Again you will need duplicates of your basics, as well as special travel items—extra business cards, pocket for itinerary, slot for dictating machine, and so on. Some cases have a fabric cover which slips over the case and enables it to double as an overnight bag.

Practise not feeling guilty if you leave your briefcase at the office at night. Why carry it around if you are not going to use the contents?

'Buckets of sweat' syndrome

An assumption that results are related to how hard you work. Not so. The good time manager knows that it's productive time—not sweat time—that matters.

Burnout

A state of physical, emotional and mental exhaustion. It is the result of fatigue and frustration brought about by dedication to a job, a cause, a way of life, or even a relationship that is not bringing the expected reward. It is accompanied by symptoms that include general malaise, feelings of helplessness and hopelessness, and a lack of enthusiasm about work and even about life in general.

Effective stress management (see **Stress**) can help prevent burnout.

Business cards

Useful reminders of business contacts. Start to order the strays by collecting them from your **desk**, shelves, drawers, **briefcase**, purse or wallet. Purchase a business card file and put them in alphabetically. Alternatively, buy special self-adhesive tabs which you can fix to cards allowing them to fit into a rotary card file.

To speed your time management further, remember to write the date and occasion on the back of the card as soon as it is handed to you. If you are busy, ask the person to write this information for you. Be aware of cultural differences though, as in Japan, for example, it is considered inappropriate to mark up a person's business card.

When you give someone your card, write the name of your assistant on the back. Then when someone calls for you, they are more likely to accept help from your assistant. This second name on your card will also make it more acceptable for your assistant to handle a call back.

18

Buy-in

Having as many people as possible involved in decision making. A buy-in is good if you're into participative decision making AND the group makes sound decisions in a reasonable amount of time. It is also good if you like meetings, as the number of meetings held is in direct proportion to the degree of buy-in.

If you use a buy-in as an excuse for everyone to get together, or as a reason to avoid taking responsibility for a decision yourself, then you are engaging in a monumental time-wasting activity.

C

C-drawer

The place where items which are low priority or unimportant can be dumped out of the way. The term was popularised by the film *The Time of Your Life* which was based on the ideas of time management author Alan Lakein (1973). He suggested that activities should be classified as A, B or C and that we can often leave many of the Cs undone. Lakein suggested that with Cs we ask ourselves, 'What can I *not* do?'. The 'nots' go into the C-drawer.

Calendar

A place to record information about activities. Calendars come in all sizes, shapes and colours and go under different names. Some hang on the wall, some sit on the desk, others go into briefcases. A **diary** can be a better time management tool.

Cassette recorder

A useful machine which can come in a container about the size of a cigarette packet. Use it to dictate notes to yourself, correspondence or draft reports. Use it in your car, on the train or in a plane. Play some motivation tapes, listen to books or learn a language while commuting. If you are trying to come to grips with a difficult presentation, record it and play it back to yourself as a memory aid.

Categories

A way of classifying material. A common use of categories for the time manager would be to help design a filing system. Grouping information into clear and simple categories is what makes a system effective.

The easiest approach to finding the right categories is to use **index cards** (colours can help). Write each item on a card and then arrange them in natural patterns, groupings or combinations. You can also use a word processing program that allows you to sort alphabetically to help devise your categories.

A good category is one you use every day and in which you can locate any paper you need in three minutes or less. *Usage*—not *storage*—should determine your categories. Remember that simple is better.

Charge-out system

A system which speeds up the location of files. Searching around for 15 or 20 minutes to find an important folder that someone has tucked into their **briefcase** is extremely frustrating for time-conscious people.

A good charge-out system means that whenever a file is taken out of the system, something is inserted in its place. Brightly coloured cards (the same size as a file folder) seem to work best. Have ruled sections on the cards with space to fill in the 'who' and the 'when'. If only a small group of people have access to the files, allocate each person their own colour for easier identification. Leave a pile of the cards on top of the files as a reminder and for easy access.

Charts

Useful forms which you can hang on the wall or put into your **diary** or file. They enable you to see relationships visually. Through the use of charts you can draw, graph, diagram, map and see the big picture as well as the details. Charts which are pre-ruled and designed for specific purposes such as time lines, calendars and expenses can be purchased in many shapes, sizes and colours.

Checklists

There are two types of checklist used in time management. The first is forms which help with organisation and **decision making**. If you find that you repeat some activity regularly, using a checklist can save you time by acting as a memory aid. For example, if you travel frequently overseas you could make up a checklist of reminders of what to do prior to the trip (e.g. update passport, get visas and health certifications) and what to take along (documents, medication, money clip, electrical adaptors, etc.). Once your list is complete, you can keep photocopies of it in your travel file.

To simplify things even further, it is possible to purchase books of prepared checklists which cover a range of needs including finances, household arrangements, car, health and travel (e.g. Carol Nichols and Jan Lurie, *Checklists*, 1981).

The second type of checklist is used to generate problem-solving ideas. First make a list of all the words and topics that you can think of which may be relevant to your problem. Daily newspapers, magazines, the Yellow Pages, brochures, handbooks will all suggest ideas. Use the list to generate ideas by yourself or duplicate it and use it at a meeting.

Children

Little people who can learn to be organised, probably from about age three. Good habits taught young will mean better habits when the children are older.

The most effective organising idea for children is to use a wall chart. This works for the very young as well as for the more 'mature' teens. As long as they can read a word or identify a picture they can use a chart.

Rule up your chart in sections, each for a basic category, and hang it in a prominent position. For young children headings like Bed, Toys, Teeth and Hair are about as complicated as they can handle. Draw (or cut from a magazine) a brightly coloured picture to represent the task and put it at the top of each section (see figure 2). Block off the sections in days and indicate 'task done' by drawing a coloured check mark or putting a coloured star in the appropriate box.

As children get older this same concept can apply not only to individual tasks, but to household chores such as gardening, window cleaning, taking out rubbish, setting the table.

To avoid fights between siblings, list all household tasks and allocate points for each task depending on degree of difficulty and time involved. Setting the table might be 1 point whereas mowing the lawn could be 20. Add up the points and divide by the number of children. Then put up your chart, with the points, indicating total points each one has to earn over the time period—say one month. Let the children agree on what they will do depending on availability, inclination, skill, etc. Tell them that if they can't agree, you will do the allocating. You can vary this approach by dividing chores into morning, evening and weekend ones and vary your points accordingly.

Figure 2   Children's wall chart

MY CHART				
	Toys	**Teeth**	**Hair**	**Bed**
Monday				
Tuesday				
Wednesday				

Chrono file

Also known as the 'chronological' or 'chron' file, this is a file arranged by date with the most recent to the front. One of the most common forms of chrono file is called the 'day file'. This contains a duplicate of every letter and memo produced. The papers are filed in 12 folders, for January through December, and then discarded month by month as the next year progresses. The file is intended as back up. If you are currently keeping a paper chronological 'day file' you are using an obsolete method. Records of almost all correspondence are now entered into computer terminals and backed up on disks. Providing you have set up your system correctly that should be all that is necessary.

Chronobiology

The study of biological body clocks. Research on this phenomenon started in 1729 and in the 1950s it was proved that body clocks exist. We all have these internal clocks which cycle continually and are as distinctive as our fingerprints. Among other things they influence waking, sleeping and eating time. (See also **Bio-rhythms**.)

Circle overlap

A way of representing the matching or mismatching of job perceptions between a manager and a team member. To check your circle overlap, think about the key responsibilities of your job and how many of your responsibilities your boss would list if asked to do so. Now draw two circles, one representing your perception and one the perception of your boss. The degree of overlap visually represents the areas of agreement between you. The lack of overlap is usually at least 25 per cent. What is the degree of non-overlap in *your* job?

To rectify this problem make a list, independently of your boss, showing major areas of responsibility and what results you think the boss expects. Ask your boss separately to prepare a similar list. Then compare the two lists. To resolve differences in perception, regularly discuss your **objectives**, **priorities**, results and methods. This will enable you both to talk about time wasting.

Circles

A useful way to set priorities at work and to resolve the sorts of conflicts that impede effective decision making is to use Stephen Covey's (1989) metaphor of concentric circles, also adopted by Roger Merrill in *Connections*.

about. This might include everything from your disapproval of your company's environmental policies to your personal goals for work for the coming year. No matter how much you care about these things, however, it may not be in your power to alter or influence them. Just as you might feel powerless to influence the policies of a multinational corporation, so your personal ambitions might be thwarted by a personal conflict with a superior.

The second circle contains the areas of your life which you know and understand, and which you *do* have the power to change. The things you *can do* in your work or personal life, however, may not necessarily harmonise with the things you really *want* out of life.

At the centre of the target are the things you are concerned about, that you have the power to influence, and that harmonise with your personal values and goals. Merrill describes this as 'the centre of your target for personal effectiveness, the "bulls eye" of the effective management of your time and resources'.

By using this circles model to set your priorities, it is argued, not only is your ability to focus your life enhanced, but your ability to influence the world around you becomes more powerful.

Cliff hangers

People who have a high need for excitement, who thrive on stress and, at the same time, create stress for everybody working with them. Cliff hangers are famed throughout an organisation because they invariably underestimate how long it will take to do something. They keep everyone around them anxious about whether they will—or will not—meet their deadlines.

There is no 'quick fix' for a cliff hanger. Correcting this habit requires a complete behaviour change. Each task needs to be planned carefully with specific, realistic time estimates. **Backwards planning** can help. **'To do' lists** with established **priorities** are essential.

As with all major behaviour change, find some simple way—if you are a cliff hanger—to reward yourself each time way—if you are a cliff hanger—to reward yourself each time you finish on time and without driving your boss and colleagues to the brink of madness.

Clustering

A right-brain 'nonlinear brainstorming process akin to free association'. Dr Gabriele Rico in *Writing the Natural Way* describes this process as one 'which allows patterns [of ideas] to emerge'. Clustering has some similarities with **mind mapping** and is a valuable technique for writing original material. If writing is difficult for you, clustering will help get your ideas on paper. It is a quick, creative and effective method.

When you are clustering, a 'nucleus word or phrase' acts as the stimulus for your writing. Write this in the centre of your page and then let your thoughts drift. Write down quickly any ideas that come to you and put them in circles. Move upwards, downwards, sideways—in any direction which feels right—linking each circle with a line. Don't take too long over any single idea. If this happens, it is your left brain trying to take over and reject this seemingly illogical process (see figure 3).

Each time you have a new notion, go back to the nucleus and link up a new cluster. After a couple of minutes, your train of thought will probably dry up. This is usually followed by the left-brain urge to make some order out of your ideas. When this happens, start writing, pulling in your various ideas from the cluster. Rico suggests that you 'read aloud what you have written'. This can help you to sense the rhythm of your writing and provide the impetus to make any modifications necessary to turn your writing into a polished piece of work.

There are no right or wrong ideas in clustering, it is whatever comes to mind in association with your key idea. Clustering is merely an idea-organising process.

Colour coding

When used sparingly, this is a practical technique for distinguishing categories—different departments, **priorities**,

Figure 3   Clustering

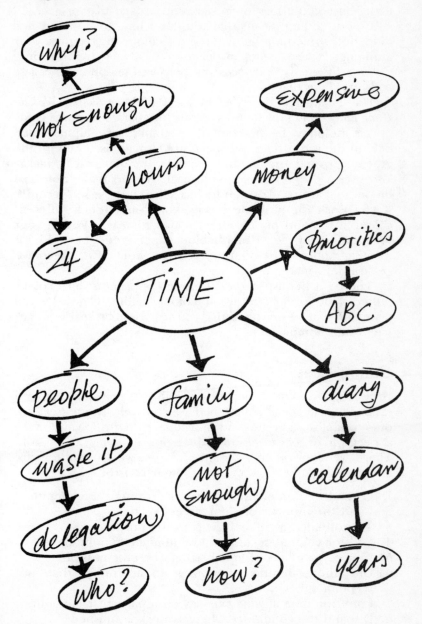

numeric breakdowns, time periods, clients, customers, products. You could also show progress in a particular project.

Colour coding means that you don't have to stop and *read* to identify something but can use the colour to recognise your **grouping**. It also assists in sorting, classifying and tracking. Coloured file covers, labels, dots, pens and telephone message pads are all available.

Harvey Mackay describes in *Swim With the Sharks, Without Being Eaten Alive* how he uses colour to separate **business cards** in his Rolodex by functions. 'Customers are alphabetised behind the red divider, prospects are alphabetised behind the green, personal friends and relatives are blue, etc.' Mackay also uses a different colour ink each year to make notes, so he can tell, at first glance, if he has talked to a person recently. If you work for multiple bosses, you could use a different coloured file and phone message pad for each. Within your organisation or department, blue paper could be used for meeting notices and minutes, red for 'hot' news, green for general information.

The right hemisphere of the brain is responsive to colour rather than 'order', so using colour coding can help you maintain systems if you think you are right-brain dominant (see **Brain dominance**).

Committees

Groups appointed or elected ostensibly to deal logically and rationally with specific matters. Unfortunately, committees are often established because an individual or a group can't make a decision or because someone wants to delay a decision. There are many other 'avoidance' reasons why committees are established. To keep committees under control:

1 Carefully consider the reason for forming the committee.
2 Limit the number of committees.
3 Try to match members' skills to the purpose.
4 Call for volunteers and avoid automatic appointments.
5 Choose members of equal status wherever possible.
6 Give the committee the power to act rather than just recommend.
7 Limit the time anyone can stay on a particular committee.
8 Disband the committee when its work is finished.

Commuting

Something that takes time and **energy**. If you commute by bus or train:

1 Use the time to get your thoughts in order for a staff meeting or appointment.
2 Do job-related reading, such as magazines, articles and newsletters.
3 Analyse personal or business problems or opportunities, and find solutions.
4 Listen to cassette tapes.
5 Pick out five good things you accomplished during the day and then feel good about going home.
6 Consider living closer to work.
7 Work from home.

Consolidation

Grouping similar activities together. This is a way of consolidating your schedule and making the best use of your time. The time management rule is 'always group like tasks'. Put **appointments**, **paperwork**, **meetings**, telephone calls into specific time blocks. You can do this on a daily or weekly basis. For example, 10–11 am could be for telephone calls and 3–4 pm for writing. Or Monday and Tuesdays could be for writing and **planning**.

Another way to consolidate is to divide time into public and private time. Remember to consider your **bio-rhythms** when **scheduling** and put those activities which are most exacting into your **prime time**. (See also **Grouping**.)

Contact file

A file which contains information about people with whom you have had contact or with whom you wish to have contact. It can form a valuable part of your time management system. Use **index cards** for your contact file or, better still, key straight into your personal computer. Contact files can store a variety of data, for example:

1 Information that is to be passed on or discussed.

2 Personal preferences, likes and dislikes, such as food or hotel preferences.
3 Names of partners or children.
4 Special insights.

Controls

A system used for monitoring delegated performance. Establishing and agreeing on controls is one of the key steps in the delegation process. Controls can be loose or tight depending on the skill and experience of the team member and the importance of the assignment. Loose controls allow almost total freedom for team members to use their initiative. Tight controls are generally used where the team member is inexperienced or when the results are particularly important.
   Controls need to be:

1 Realistically based on what the person is currently likely to achieve.
2 Simple.
3 Understood and agreed to by everyone involved.
4 Directly observable—by anyone—and not biased or designed for failure.
5 Consistent.
6 Appropriate for the results expected.

In designing your control system, have a mechanism which allows a control to be corrected if circumstances change, or if the control proves to be inappropriate. Always make allowances in case something happens which is outside the control of the team member. Have a systematic way of monitoring the task. Monitoring methods include personal follow-up, regular progress reports, sampling of work and comparisons with previous performance. (See also **Delegation**.)

Cooperative reading

If you know readers who have interests similar to your own, why not establish a reading cooperative? You only need six to eight members who each agree to read their share (one-sixth/one-eighth) of the journals, articles or books in your common interest areas. Then once or twice a month you hold your cooperative meetings and each member tells about the worthwhile items they have read. Members also can agree to provide reference information for anyone who wants to follow up and read the original.

It may take a while until the membership of your cooperative stabilises but be patient. The time saved is worth the effort. If your cooperative is based on an organisation or department, it's not bad for inter-office communications either.

Crisis management

Management by fire, flood and famine. Good time managers don't have crises. They practise crisis *prevention* methods recognising that this is preferable to 'fire fighting' and remedial action.

Most crises are 'manufactured'. The crisis maker is emotional and enjoys involving as many people as possible in the excitement. If you are crisis-prone your days need to be filled with variety—both inside and outside work. If you become bored, you will be out looking for a crisis to happen.

If you seem to be having too many crises, start logging (see **Time log**) and categorising them. Look for patterns. Analyse the sources, causes, seriousness and controllable factors. Find out how many of the crises are really unique and how many are your fault. Once you have your log, you can develop contingency plans and begin practising crisis prevention. Some useful techniques:

1 Recognise that there is a problem.
2 Set clear goals and plan your work.
3 Follow your plan. This may sound obvious but crisis makers love deviating from their plan. This increases their excitement level.
4 Give a team member the role of *crisis prevention ombudsman*. Give your ombudsman the power to take preventative or corrective action and encourage team members to report potential crises to the ombudsman as early as possible. Ask the ombudsman to report at regular staff meetings with a suggested dollar figure for the cost of each crisis.
5 Have agreed team definitions of what is meant by terms such as 'urgent'.

6 Devise a detailed schedule for all large projects, and check the schedule regularly with your team.
7 Review each crisis afterwards to see what caused it, what you did and what could have prevented it.

Critique

A way to learn from experience. It is particularly effective in helping to save time and to improve the quality of decision making at meetings. To critique a meeting involves evaluating it in a thoughtful way before, during and after it has been completed. Blake and Mouton in *Making Experience Work*, and in their books on the 'Managerial Grid', say that the purpose of critique is to:

1 Identify processes, actions or procedures which facilitate team effectiveness.
2 Identify problems of team effectiveness.
3 Set up ground rules and standards for the future.

To establish a simple critiquing process, team members need to agree to be open and candid about how they feel about what is going on at the meeting and to confront conflict. For effective critique, the team should look at three areas:

1 *Process.* **Planning**, leading, time management, team member participation, conduct of individuals.
2 *Content.* People's opinions, expertise, information, suggestions, data.
3 *Feelings.* Expression of feelings, checking for feelings, acknowledging others' feelings.

Before the 'formal' business of the meeting commences, start the critique by reviewing the planning process. Discuss the way the Agenda has been formulated and how and by whom the meeting is to be chaired. Agree to critique during the meeting at regular intervals. Depending on the length of the meeting this could be every half hour or every hour. Appoint a time-keeper who will remind the group when it is time to critique.
During the meeting, when the item for the critique arrives, stop the meeting and discuss how people are feeling about the process and the content of the meeting. Listen carefully

to all comments and, if necessary, suggest changes in the meeting process.

After the meeting, hold a 'post mortem'. Ask what could have been done differently. Agree on new ground rules for the next meeting.

While it may seem a lengthy process, once the team is experienced in using the technique a simple but effective critique can be done in 5 minutes. The activity may be the most valuable and time-saving outcome of your meeting.

Cross referencing

A way of speeding up the search for documents by putting a reference in a second (or third) place when a document relates to more than one information category.

Looking for lost documents is one of the biggest time wasters around. The problem is that it is often difficult to know which of two or more possible category names or subjects is the more important. To make sure the document can be found, file the original under one name and prepare a cross reference under another. If you are using paper files, printed forms can be used for cross reference sheets—or plain pages of coloured paper. If your documents are on computer, put a cross reference note in your computer index.

Cultural time

Differences in time perceptions in different cultures. Western society adheres to mechanical time almost religiously. For us, 10 am means 10 am. That is not necessarily true for the rest of the world. In some countries an appointment time is seen as merely giving some idea of when a meeting might be held. The expression 'rubber time', for example, is very common in some countries and refers to the way the locals use their time. To avoid frustration when travelling, make allowances in your schedule for 'rubber time'.

D

D & I chart

A chart used to look for pressure points in the work day and to 'try to keep track of demands (D) and interruptions (I)'. This is another form of logging (see **Time log**). You can devise your own recording system. A section of your **diary** would be convenient and easy to follow. This is also another good use for **index cards**.

Consultant Dr Dru Scott writing in *How to Put More Time in Your Life*, says that whenever a demand or interruption occurs you should make a note of the '*when, who* and *what*'. Then search for patterns. Who are the demands and interruptions coming from? Is it often/always the same people? Are they coming at certain times of the day? Can more or different information be transmitted to people at **meetings** or by memo? Working on this technique for even a short time and then taking remedial action, can help eliminate unnecessary **interruptions**.

Deadline

The designated time when something is supposed to be finished. Whenever a project or task is allocated it deserves a deadline. You should be able to estimate a completion time within—at most—a 5 to 10 per cent margin for error.

The capacity to meet deadlines seems to elude some people. Sometimes the problem lies with the *setting* of the deadline itself. It is better to negotiate a more realistic deadline at the beginning of a project than to suffer the results of a deadline which has not been met. When you are doing your own **planning**, always make allowances for other people's deadlines.

Decidophobia

An ailment you have when you are incapable of making decisions at all and even the simplest priority seems overwhelming. If you are decidophobic, learn to recognise what prevents you from making decisions and try to develop a good decision making system (see **Procrastination**).

Decision making

The act of determining what should happen next. Decision making touches nearly everything you do. Whether decisions are minor, major, carefully planned or spontaneous, they are made every day. That is, of course, unless you are suffering from **decidophobia**. There are many reasons why you sometimes fail to make decisions. Fear of failure, paralysis by analysis, inability to take risks, 'waiting for the right time' and **procrastination** are the most common.

Good decision making begins with doing proper research and evaluating the risks. If you have a decision to make which requires ranking items in order of priority, use a matrix arranging the items in sets in a table. Working your way carefully through these ten questions may help:

1 If you proceed with the decision will you succeed?
2 What is the likely result?
3 Is it worth it?
4 What are the chances of the result occurring?
5 If you put it off will the result be a loss or a gain?
6 If the result does occur, what weight would you give to the loss?
7 What weight would you give to the gain?
8 What alternative gives you the best edge?
9 If there is no good alternative, should you do nothing?
10 What are the risks?

When all else fails, here are two 'quick fix' tactics. The first is to sit quietly at your desk, close your eyes, take a few deep breaths and ask yourself this question: 'What would the World's Greatest Authority do in this situation?'. When the answer comes (and it will), do it!

The second tactic is to put decisions into one of two

categories: 'easily fixed' (few resources and little time required) or 'difficult to fix' (expensive in terms of time, money, human resources, etc.). Once you have categorised your decision, delegate the 'easily fixed' and spend your time fixing the 'difficult'.

Although making a decision by yourself may be the fastest method of decision making, it may not be the best. Decisions can be made by group consensus, by majority vote or by averaging individual opinions. Using one of these methods may mean more time initially but, by involving others in the decision, there is likely to be more cooperation and less risk of sabotage of the decision.

Beware of *default decision making*. This is a close relative of **reverse delegation**. When it occurs your team member has *you* making all the decisions rather than taking the risk and responsibility themself. This means that they miss out on the experience that comes with taking responsibility for the decisions, as well as not being accountable for errors.

Delegation

Entrusting power and authority to a team member to act on your behalf. The team member acts as your 'agent' or representative and has responsibility for performing a defined task or activity. Delegation is the essence of management. The success of delegation depends as much on closeness and team spirit as it does on the skill of the delegator and the team member.

Delegation makes good business sense. For starters it increases job satisfaction, provides variety and novelty, develops skills and increases promotion potential. It also multiplies productivity and means faster, more effective decisions at the appropriate level. Here are ten cardinal rules of delegation:

1 Do nothing yourself that you can delegate.
2 Delegate tasks you thought only you could do.
3 Delegate to the most junior person with the skills and rank.
4 Delegate authority as well as responsibility.
5 If you don't have someone to delegate to, find them and train them.

6 Delegate in progressive phases or degrees to allow for review and revision.
7 Try to parcel out the work early each day (or week or whatever period of time is relevant).
8 Focus on results and give freedom of action, avoiding 'have to' and 'should'.
9 *Always* acknowledge and give credit to the person who has done the job.
10 Know what not to delegate (see below).

Figure 4   Delegation chart

DELEGATION REMINDERS	
Categorise jobs into:	1 can wholly assign 2 can partly assign 3 have to do myself
Things you can delegate are:	1 tasks 2 functions 3 skills
When you are delegating, consider:	1 skill 2 interest 3 workload
Managers and supervisors waste their team members' time by:	1 poor instructions 2 keeping them waiting 3 interrupting their work

Poor delegators show many symptoms. Which of these 25 are you exhibiting now?

1 Need to know all the details.
2 'I can do it better myself' illusion.
3 Lack of experience in delegating.
4 Insecurity.
5 Poor planning.
6 Lack of objectives.
7 Slow decision making.
8 Too large a span of control.
9 Believe delegating is a sign of weakness.
10 Fear of loss of control.

11 Constant pressure and confusion.
12 It doesn't occur to you.
13 'My boss won't let me' syndrome.
14 Disinclined to develop team members.
15 Lack of organisational skills.
16 Fear of being disliked.
17 Too busy to delegate.
18 Lack of policy or too much policy.
19 Want to do it yourself.
20 Want to feel indispensable.
21 Perfectionism.
22 Lack of confidence in team members.
23 Fear of mistakes.
24 'Workers don't want responsibility' fallacy.
25 'No one else has the experience' misconception.

Of course it is not always the direct or immediate fault of the manager when a team member does not handle delegation effectively. The team member may prove to lack experience, be overloaded with work, want to avoid responsibility, be disorganised, be immersed in trivia, be overdependent on the boss, or just lack competence. Here are ten steps to effective delegation:

1 Define the goal succinctly.
2 Select the person.
3 Discuss the scope of the job and how it can be done.
4 Agree on approach.
5 Agree on authority and responsibility.
6 Agree on limitations, boundaries, parameters and resources.
7 Establish controls, progress checkpoints and reporting mechanisms.
8 Agree on time schedules and deadlines.
9 Agree on way of measuring performance.
10 Follow through: discuss, give feedback, coach and counsel if necessary.

If controls show that performance is unsatisfactory the manager needs to intervene and take corrective action. There may be a warning or a reprimand in serious cases. This may be followed by rescinding authority or reassigning tasks.

There are some things which generally should not be

delegated. They are disciplinary action, performance evaluation, counselling and morale problems, and confidential matters.

Warning! Don't fall for the 'replacement myth'. This perpetuates the belief that a team member who does a good job will end up replacing or surpassing you. Part of your job is to train your employees for promotion and to get the best results possible. High level performance by staff is a credit to a manager and allows you to bask in the light of reflected glory.

Desk

Work space not storage space. Sensible desk control is essential in time management. The desk is basically a reading, writing and sorting surface. Exceptions include the **telephone**, teledex, note pad, **diary**, clock with timer, in/out baskets, writing implements and a **desk workbook**. Papers, food, trophies all belong somewhere else.

Size, shape, angle(s), location and lighting all influence how well you work at your desk. If you have the privilege of choosing your own desk, explore the possibilities of modular furniture. Consider the advantages and disadvantages of L-shape, U-shape and J-shape. Two work surfaces with accessible storage for frequently used items are ideal. The surface in front of you is your primary work space. Off to one side you need space for computer, telephone or storage or for items used frequently.

Arrange the layout to suit your own comfort level and to minimise distractions. Having your back or side to visitors will help decrease the number of 'drop-ins'. In open offices, a strategically placed partition or bushy plant can help limit distractions. Try not to work facing a window and have a comfortable chair which is appropriate for the type of work you do.

Paperwork flow on your desk should be U-shaped. For right-handed people, incoming mail and messages go in the upper right-hand corner. As they are actioned they go to your work space. If items are 'pending' they should go in files in your desk on the right side. Items completed go to the out basket in the top left-hand corner. Left-handed people may wish to reverse this flow.

Use good **accessories**, e.g. clear or translucent plastic desk trays, pencil containers. Use alphabetised telephone/address books. Carefully consider how you might use the wall space near your desk. Slanted hanging racks for storage and whiteboards for planning are time and space efficient. Leave 3 to 5 minutes at the end of each day for desk cleanup. Remove as many items as possible, put material into in/out baskets or your **desk workbook**, store staplers and similar in a drawer. As you lift every item ask, 'What is the worst thing that will happen if I throw this away?'. If you can live without it, dump it. (See also **G.U.T.S.**)

Desk workbook

A looseleaf folder which contains all the pieces of paper you think you might need later: instruction leaflets for equipment, travel notes, ideas you are working on, etc. Rather than having these items scattered or stored all over the desk, punch some holes in the side and secure them into your looseleaf folder. You will know where they are when you want them.

Desktop scan

A method used to help clear and sort materials from a desk top to turn it into work space rather than storage space. To conduct the scan draw up a chart as in figure 5 and list all the things that are currently on your desk, categorising them according to those used daily, weekly, monthly, yearly or very rarely.

Figure 5   Desktop scan

Daily	Weekly	Monthly	Yearly	Occasion-ally	Almost never

Once you have identified the different groups, put the items used most frequently in your immediate work area. Put those things you use for a particular activity (calculating, telephoning) off to a side. Store or file other items but, as you do, ask of each item, 'What is the worst thing that will happen if I throw this away?'. If the answer is 'not much', throw it away.

Diary

An essential for anyone who wants to be time-conscious. Selecting a diary is serious business. Size, shape, colour and texture all have a bearing on the choice. Diaries don't have to be expensive but they do have to fit your style and your life. Choose one you will enjoy using because you will be looking at it frequently.

Choose a diary which is small enough to carry with you but large enough to record all the details you need. Find a size that suits your work level and your appointment load. A diary which also has room for a **'to do' list** can be useful. If it hasn't, try ruling a line down the centre of each page and using one half for the list.

What works for *you* is what is important. Different page layouts suit different working styles. People who are strongly right-brain dominant benefit from a diary which appeals to their imagination.

If you wish to go to the top end of the market, there are elaborate planners available with space for appointments, notes, phone directories, expense reports and even an envelope for receipts. But purchasing an expensive diary which sits in a drawer is not effective time or money management.

If you like taking risks with your time, by all means use several diaries. Then live with the excitement which comes from having important information omitted from one of your collection. It might be better, unless you have a very reliable assistant or a foolproof routine, to find *one* diary in which to list all appointments, events and deadlines. Don't be tempted when your friendly neighbourhood salesperson gives you a second diary, even if it is the latest model in antelope hide with an embossed logo on the cover. These make welcome presents for artistic children.

Some people reject diaries entirely because they fear that their lives may become too rigid or that their time isn't worth enough to write anything down about it. This can also make for an exciting—if perilous—lifestyle. In reality the diary doesn't *control* you, it *frees* you and enables you to relax and avoid worrying whether you will remember your next appointment. Some people call this 'delegating on paper'.

Your diary is a helping and **planning** tool, not just a place to record **appointments**. Jotting down brief notes when making an appointment can act as a useful prompt before a meeting. Making appointments with yourself for quiet work time is also a valuable way to use your diary.

Dictation

Using your voice to communicate notes, memos, letters or instructions via a tape or to a shorthand writer. Dictate any items that would take longer than 5 to 10 minutes to write. Dictation is one of the most effective means of saving time. We talk at speeds between 150 and 275 words a minute, whereas we write at 20 to 30 words a minute. A good assistant can take shorthand at 100 words per minute. So 1 hour of dictation equals about 5 hours of writing.

If using a tape recorder, select one that is light, compact, voice-activated and fits in your hand. Features may include a clock, timer modes, alarm and tape counter. You can record instructions and have people report to you on tape. You can also read important items, speech notes or articles onto tapes and listen while driving and dressing. Apply some sensible systems to your dictation. If tapes are your preference for dictation, use different tapes for different purposes and try coloured labels to signal the purpose. If an instruction checklist does not exist, design one to suit your needs. Include these items: your name, type of dictation (letter, instructions, memo, report, etc.), priority, draft or final copy, paper to be used, names of people receiving copies, enclosures, signature, approximate length of item and any special instructions.

Whether you use tape or face-to-face dictation, unless you know exactly what you want to say, make a rough outline before you start. Each re-draft is a cost in both time and money for you and for the transcriber. Speak distinctly and enunciate clearly using a conversational tone and a steady pace. Try to modulate your voice so that the listener can tell the difference between instructions and the message. Spell unusual or technical words and dictate special punctuation, spacing changes, underlining and new paragraphs.

Discomfort dodging

Avoiding tasks entirely because they are associated with feelings of anxiety or irritability. Have you put off writing a financial report recently? Is it because you dislike anything to do with numbers? Are you still neglecting to draft that speech? Maybe you really hate public speaking.

Avoiding a project because you want to avoid the associated discomfort will get you nowhere—literally. Try to come to terms with what is causing the discomfort and confront it. Take a course in coping with maths anxiety, join Toastmasters or Toastmistresses or other clubs such as Penguin which have as their objectives improving public speaking as well as networking. Work with a team member who has the skills you lack. If you continue to dodge the discomfort you can expect some reactions. These may come from your boss at performance appraisal time, or from your stomach when you start showing symptoms of an ulcer. Act now!

Discretionary time

The time of which we never have enough! The reason? Most people tend to overprogram, scattering **appointments** and **meetings** at random all through the week. If you are not a believer, keep a simple **time log** and see.

A possible solution? **Block in** large sections of time during your week—half-days or days are ideal—and schedule similar activities into those blocks. Try to consolidate travel, meetings, staff consultations and other time-consuming activities. The more you block in 'like' tasks, the more discretionary time will become available to you.

Doubling up

Any two (or more) activities you can do simultaneously. Exercise while watching TV. Listen to a tape on international finance while driving. Read reports while waiting for an appointment. Sign letters during a meeting. Do knee bends while brushing your teeth. It's easy. Anything you can double up on saves you half the time.

Drop-in visitors

Uninvited visitors who interrupt your work. Some of these 'techniques' may help cut down on the traffic:

1 Allow an interruption if it can be dealt with in one minute. Look at your watch when you start and say 'go'.
2 Stand up and move out from behind your desk when someone comes into your office or work space.
3 Collect some papers, keys, folders from your desk and walk towards the door after a few minutes.
4 Delegate **interruptions**.
5 Cover chairs with papers.
6 Remove chairs.
7 If you see an interrupter coming meet them outside your office.
8 Have a clock in full view.
9 Get visitors screened.
10 Arrange your desk so that your back is towards the door.
11 Find a 'hide out'.

When all else fails, try hanging some of the 'signs of interruption' in figure 6 on your door (or on the corner of your desk if you have no door). One efficient time manager had a battery-operated red panel light installed on the door. (See also **Interruptions**.)

Dual career couples

Couples who live together while both hold full-time jobs. This creates time constraints on both partners who find that they are overloaded with work and confused about the demands

Figure 6   Signs of interruption

made upon them by their dual roles. Of course, the usual time management principles apply to dual career couples as well as to anyone else. Here are some extra suggestions:

1 Seriously look at the demands on your time, and each time you are confronted with a chore ask: 'Do I/we really have to do this?'. For example, is ironing of sheets and towels a must?

2 Agree on some rules about when you will talk together when it is *not about work*.

3 Spend money to save time—and **energy**. Look for cleaning and gardening help. Dishwashing machines are a must.

4 Plan time to relax—together and separately. Personal space and time is an important part of **stress** reduction.

5 Decide how you will deal with social and business invitations. Agree to consult on all invitations either of you receive or try some new strategies. One successful dual couple have agreed that Monday to Thursday they 'do their own thing' including finding their own dinner. From Friday dinner until 9 am Monday they do things as a couple and share all chores.

6 If you are changing residence, look for a house or flat that has 'easy-care' features. If you hate gardening don't buy a 10 hectare property.

7 Entertain by sharing a dinner. Have each guest/couple provide one course while you provide table, wine and dessert. Or invite guests for dessert only.

8 If you cook, try to double or triple the recipe; ask a gourmet neighbour to cook extra meals for a small sum for you to freeze; stop feeling guilty about take-away food.

Many of the time pressures and causes of friction arise from uneven sharing of household and childcare chores. Men and women see 'mess' differently, and 'most women' have detailed household-management maps in their heads. Many men, and most children, however, haven't the faintest idea of what is really involved in keeping a house functioning.

Marjorie and Morton Shaevitz in *Making it Together* suggest that one solution which can rescue one partner from being overworked is to prepare an inventory of all 'household management' tasks and services. This includes 'all those responsibilities, tasks, and services required to maintain a couple and their dependants in a home'. They go on to classify items under these headings:

House cleaning, house maintenance, children-related activities, meals and food, clothing, indoor and outdoor plants and garden, cars, bill paying and financial management, health-related activities (doctors, dentists), family and social relationships and events, holiday-related activities, religious activities, pets and emergencies.

Once you have compiled your inventory, everyone needs to concur on acceptable standards *and* 'the all-important who'. 'No one person in your household should become a sacrificial lamb', the Shaevitz's say. The last step is to get all contributors to rank each inventory item on a scale of 10 according to their availability, their level of skill and their enjoyment. Then negotiate on who will do what.

E

Efficiency v. effectiveness

Two terms which are often confused. Being effective is choosing the right **goals/objectives** from a set of alternatives, and reaching those goals/objectives. Being efficient means assuming that the goals/objectives are correct, and achieving them with the least—or a low—expenditure of effort or resources.

Eighty–twenty rule

An often misused and abused concept proposed by a 19th century Italian economist and sociologist, Vilfredo Pareto. It is also known as **Pareto's principle**.

Pareto observed that 'the *significant items* in a given group normally constitute a relatively small portion of the total items in the group'. In positive terms, this means that a small portion of your activities are vital and these contribute the most towards your purposes. That seems to make good sense, but it works both ways. For example: the bulk of absenteeism in an organisation is accounted for by a relatively small number of employees; a few quality characteristics in a product account for the major number of quality inspection rejects; 20 per cent of a product line produces 80 per cent of the total sales; at meetings a few of the people do most of the talking.

Pareto's Principle, however, is just an *observation* and there may be risks in applying it too rigidly. Look again at the 20 per cent of a product line which produces 80 per cent of sales. Your salespeople might be wise to drop some customers and concentrate on the best 20 per cent. But the problem with applying the Eighty–twenty rule too rigidly is that they may soon end up with very few accounts.

Just the same, it is useful to apply this observation to time management. Ask yourself how much time you spend on the 20 per cent of your activities that produce the high payoffs. Could you see fewer visitors? Delegate more minor tasks? Concentrate on the most strategic assignments? Pareto's Principle can be helpful in forcing you to focus on that handful of things which will ultimately make the most significant contribution to your productivity.

Electronic mail

A computer- and communications-based interoffice mail system. For some managers and administrators, electronic mail (E-mail) is the first and main use for data terminals in communicating workstations. E-mail can be very time saving and is seen to be far quicker than normal interoffice or external postal systems.

The operation is quite simple. From a video terminal in any office the user can enter a message, with a short subject heading, together with the name of a recipient (or list of recipients). The mail can be private ('eyes only') or regular. Service is immediate. Only a few minutes elapse before the distribution system has received the mail, sorted it, and made it available to the destinations. Different software systems exist, and most see to it that users are told at log-in or log-out time that mail is waiting. Also, systems can immediately alert the user to the arrival of new mail.

Elephant eating

The lofty elephant is used to symbolise your most substantial, high priority goals. Just as it is very difficult to eat an elephant at one meal, so it is frequently impossible to deal with a high payoff goal in one sitting. To prevent time being squandered on inviting but less substantial meals select the part of the elephant you want to eat each day, and start chewing. How many of *your* elephants are now waiting in the freezer?

Elevator time

The way to capture a few valuable minutes each day if you work high up in a tall building. If you get restless and irritable while waiting for elevators or lifts and if this is a daily occurrence, Stephanie Winston, author of *Getting Organized*, suggests you 'plan ahead, so that you have with you the tools you need to accomplish something'. Use your mobile phone for a short call and the mirror (there usually is one) to straighten your hair, tie or blouse. 'Carry a list of things to do and a small tape recorder. Dictate letters (short thank-you notes, etc.) or random thoughts about how to approach certain problems.' Update your 'to do' or shopping list. If you are by yourself, do some knee bends . . . Better still, use the stairs. As well as giving you some exercise it will help relieve the stress you experienced while waiting for the elevator.

Elimination principle

The principle of abolishing, deleting or obliterating from your own, your team's and your organisation's life any work that no longer contributes to primary goals. Most people fall into the trap of continuing to do tasks long after they have served any useful purpose. Some tasks may have been inherited from previous job incumbents (or from the company founder, circa 1927). These should also be subject to the elimination principle. (See also **Last, job leftovers**.)

Sydney Love in *Mastery and Management of Time* suggests that you start to 'question any regular routine activity'. Then ask yourself: How is this activity contributing to our productivity? If we stop doing it will it make any difference? To whom? To what? Why? Sydney Love says that we need to learn to 'say "no"—be polite, explain, but be firm' to new requests for time unless they can pass the elimination test. This principle applies equally well to all your **meetings**.

Energy

Something which creates *more* energy. Research shows that we get energy from excitement, positive stress, doing new things, being creative, day-dreaming, being passionate, taking a risk, relaxing, having a challenge, being optimistic, exercising, being committed to goals, having a healthy work environment, and balancing work and 'play'. How many of these things are in your life right now?

You can gain more energy by:

1 Getting in touch with your body clock and learning to organise high energy tasks in high energy periods and vice versa.
2 Recognising Type A influences and learning to hasten slowly (see **Type A behaviour**).
3 Building variety into your day and taking time off for **joy breaks**.
4 Alternating physical exercise with desk work.
5 Doing nothing on a regular basis.
6 Taking regular long holidays, and frequent short ones.
7 Making your office surroundings as pleasant and enjoyable as possible.
8 Having a supportive network of friends.
9 Coming to work early, and giving the day a headstart.
10 Giving someone positive feedback—about anything.

Environment

The physical surroundings in which you work; the way in which work area organisation, light, colour, sound, furniture, atmospheric conditions, walls, doors and openings in an office fit together.

How comfortable are you feeling about your office space? Does your space reflect your personality? Do you have some objects you love around you—or is it just boring work space? Even if you only spend one day a week in your work space that's 20 per cent of your time. So why not create an environment that's welcoming and aesthetically pleasing? It won't hurt your time management.

Colour, temperature, lighting, airborne toxins such as smoke, safety features, privacy—all influence **productivity**. The atmosphere of your surroundings affects how you feel as well as how others perceive you. Designing and arranging a successful time-conscious office is a complex task but is worth the effort. Higher productivity and feelings of comfort, pleasure, enjoyment, importance and energy can result.

Work habits need to be analysed and consideration given to physiological needs (posture, movement, eyestrain, fatigue, general comfort) as well as psychosocial needs (nature of work, break schedules, work flow, privacy, security).

Work space and storage space and all physical objects need to be functionally related to one another. All this must be considered with your budget in mind. When designing your office layout consider location, space, access and comfort. Those items which are most often used need to be close by and configured to meet needs of co-workers, clients and customers. Similar items need to be grouped together, and space used to create different areas for each of the tasks you do.

You can create an environment which gives you strength, stamina and energy by creating high energy surroundings. Colours, plants and flowers, photographs, posters and executive 'toys' all help.

When planning work areas, consider atmospheric conditions (including lighting; noise; all appropriate desks, chairs and other furniture).

Equipment overload

A syndrome which is easily identified by looking at someone's desktop. Is it covered with pens, stapler, calculator, hole punch, tape dispenser, correcting fluid, scissors etc.? The solution? Commit this ditty to memory and put it into practice: 'Put it all in a drawer, that is what it is for'.

Ergonomics

The science of making a work environment compatible with the people. The result is that they work in greater comfort, with increased productivity, and with better time management.

Some of the symptoms of poor ergonomics are excessive fatigue, eyestrain, headaches, stiff muscles, blurred vision and repetition strain injury (RSI). All of these symptoms can have an effect on usage of time. Ergonomic planning also looks at dimensions of furniture and equipment (tables, chairs, desks, computer terminals) and matches them to approved standards.

Estimating

A way to improve your ability to accurately estimate how much time you need to complete particular tasks. As you organise your week, jot down beside each activity how much time you *think* it will take to complete them. Then jot down the time it *actually* took. As you do this you will gradually become more accurate at estimating—and thus better at **planning** your time usage and managing your **diary**.

Everything out

People who suffer from this syndrome say 'they work best when everything they need is out in front of them'. Sunny Schlenger and Roberta Roesch in *How to be Organized in Spite of Yourself* believe that the 'everything out' person thinks that this saves time. What a waste it is to put something away as you will probably need it tomorrow anyhow. After all, inspiration comes from seeing things around you.

If you are strongly right-brain dominant (see **Brain dominance**) you will almost inevitably be an 'everything out' person. A regular **desktop scan** is one strategy which can help. Schlenger and Roesch also suggest working out a good 'basic sorting system for your incoming paperwork'. Have the right **accessories**, use **colour coding**, and 'make effective use of wall space for storage and display'.

F

Fax

A machine used for transmitting written, printed or pictorial documents via the telephone system. Most time managers love using their fax machines. A word of caution however. While you might perceive your decision to send a message by fax as important, urgent or helpful, the person who receives it is likely to see it as less critical. In other words, we value the messages we send more than the ones we receive—and we act accordingly.

Fear of failure

The reason we often procrastinate or refuse to take a high payoff risk. This fear can present itself in many ways: fear of the unknown, fear of self-disclosure, fear of confrontation, fear of not meeting our own perfectionist standards.

Fear of failure immobilises you and allows you to take the easy way out. It also provides a false sense of security as you can't lose a race you haven't entered. As well as showing up in poor time management practices, fear of failure can manifest itself in an increase in drinking and eating, vague physical symptoms or a pretence that the problem doesn't really exist.

It's important to remember that 'failure' is an arbitrary thing—merely an opinion. It needs to be based on your own standards and not those set down by others. Excellence in everything is probably not possible and, in terms of time management, not necessarily desirable. Recognise that failure is a learning experience and benefit by knowing what you will do differently next time. Significant success rarely comes without a struggle.

Imaging or creative **visualisation** can help. Think about

yourself doing what you want to do *successfully*. Value your own performance and meet failure head on. Start small, and build on each little success to overcome the fear.

Fence sitter

Someone who leaves everything to chance because they can't make a decision and prefer sitting on the fence. This is a very precarious time management position, especially if the fence is pointed or made from barbed wire.

'Should I or shouldn't I?'. 'Yes or no?'. Back and forth. All this means is that you will seldom achieve what you want to achieve and others will probably end up making the decision for you. Inability to rank **priorities** because there are many choices available is also fence sitting.

For help, attend a **decision-making** program. Develop a sound priority system and set firm decision deadlines. If you're desperate, flip a coin or use one of those 'executive decision makers' with a dial that you can spin to either 'yes' or 'no'. Remember that, whatever the outcome, at least you will have made the decision to act. Most people agree that they would rather work for someone who makes some mistakes than for someone who never decides.

File spread

Worse than middle-age spread. *That* spread you see only when you look in the mirror. File spread you see every time you look at your desk. Remember that 'file' is also a verb. Many people work best with the fewest distractions possible. Of course, right-brain dominant people (see **Brain dominance**) need the files out because they are afraid they will forget about them. They also provide some stimulation. For files which *need* to remain close by (for whatever reason) at least have them labelled, organised and closed. Otherwise use the **C-drawer** or put files in the cabinet where they belong.

Filing

A way of sorting and storing information. Even in these days of computerisation, most people still keep paper files. With either paper or electronic storage systems, *easy access to information* is the point of filing. Three minutes should be the maximum retrieval time. *Usage* not storage is the key to establishing a good system.

Start by setting up a system that is simple and useable. Retrieval—not filing—should be easy. Alphabetic systems are the most popular, followed by chronological (see **Chrono file**) and numerical. Numerical files usually need an alphabetic index which can duplicate effort. Look for clear, simple, broad generic **categories** and sub-categories. Write them out on paper first to 'test' them and then circulate to potential users for their views.

If using paper files, the type and style of storage cabinets you use will depend on frequency of use, required size, shape and quality of documents, and also your need for proximity to the documents.

To maintain your paper system and keep it up to date, follow some simple rules:

1 File don't pile. Ten to twelve papers is the maximum for a pile.
2 Decide who will file what and for how long.
3 When in doubt, throw it out. Keep items that are original efforts, can't easily be duplicated, that you expect to refer to, and can't get elsewhere.
4 Classify into 'active', 'inactive' and 'dead' and store accordingly; identify how long something will be needed, being conscious of the legal requirements.
5 **Colour code** your files.
6 File the most recent paper in front (including copies). Use staples not paper clips. Clips get lost and have a habit of latching on to other papers.
7 Draw up an index and paste it on the front of the cabinet or place it in an easy access index file.
8 Have a good **charge out system**.
9 Divide larger files into smaller groups to avoid overspill.
10 Don't keep something in your file if someone else can keep it in theirs.

11 Use **cross references** not duplicates.
12 If you are using a file put each item back where you got it as soon as you are done with it, and put the file back where you found it.

Lateral files take up more space than vertical files and open only 89 cm (35 inches) compared to 137 cm (54 inches). For a busy system, front-filled laterals are easier for access and manila or hanging files the best.

Each time you look into a file, spend a minute or so sifting through it and throwing away the excess. When cleaning out, limit yourself to one file or drawer at a time. To help keep your desk clear have a few files with labels like 'ideas, 'rough projects' or 'plans', and keep 'miscellaneous' files at your peril.

Financial master list

A valuable list which helps to unscramble financial information under a variety of circumstances, e.g. if a credit card or document is mislaid or stolen. To start your financial master list, type—or write down—all your important numbers: bank account, credit cards, drivers licence, insurance policies, stocks, share certificates, and so on. Then add to that list the name, address and telephone number of your accountant and your solicitor. Note any special financial obligations, properties owned, investments held, superannuation, and location of safe deposit box, will and any personal papers.

Make three copies of the list and keep one in a fireproof box, one in your safe deposit box and one in your 'important documents' file.

Flowchart

A chart or diagram which translates tasks into visual form, with limited narrative description. It can be used to show all of the key steps in a work procedure or system, to track recurring tasks or to monitor time.

There are three most commonly used symbols in standard flowcharts. The first symbol represents the start or stop of the procedure, the second represents an operation, the third represents a decision. Flowlines, which indicate the direction of movement, are used to connect symbols of a flowchart (see figure 7).

A flowcharting template is very useful for flowcharts as it includes the most commonly used symbols plus all the other symbols used. If you will be doing a good deal of flowcharting, there are computer software packages available which enable you to reproduce charts very quickly.

Follow-up system

A sorting system to remind you of tasks and dates. Usually called a follow-up or tickler system, the first essential is that the system works for *you*. The stronger your right-brain preference (see **Brain dominance**), the harder it will be to find the one right system.

If you are computer-competent, there are many software packages which have features to help you follow up. For example, *Windows* has a reminder note which pops into the screen when you start your program each day. You can find systems with alarms and other reminder capabilities, so check out the latest software. Many organisations have purchased computer systems with an in-built follow-up feature.

Time management diaries frequently have special follow-up features. With the most simple system, the desk **calendar**, simply jot reminder notes on your calendar and then place any documents relevant to that task or date into the appropriate file. For an alternative paper-based system use letter-sized files or **index cards**.

For a letter-sized follow-up system, you will need 48 file folders. Label one folder for each day of the month (1–31), one for each month of the year (Jan–Dec) and one for each of the next 5 years (1993–1997). Arrange them in order: day, month and year. As tasks come to hand that will need to be followed up, put relevant letters/reminder notes/telephone messages/flight tickets/meeting papers into the file according to the date you need to follow up.

You may prefer to use index cards. Use section dividers for your card file, labelled in a similar fashion to the letter-sized follow-up system (days, months, years). Carry a supply of index cards with you (some people put them in every room and every drawer) and jot reminders on the cards. File them

Figure 7 Flowchart

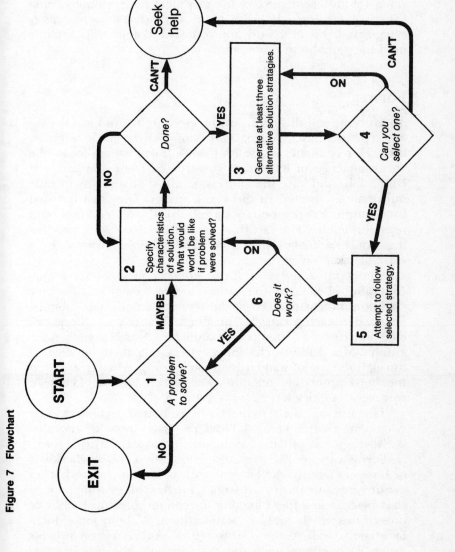

behind the appropriate divider. Have blank cards behind each divider and use them to note follow-up items as you would with your desk calendar.

Many clever systems have been designed using coloured cards for different purposes, e.g. yellow for customers, blue for projects, etc. If your main activities can be easily categorised this may work for you. The colour will certainly help the right-brain dominants.

Forms

An efficient and simple means of speeding up and standardising repetitive tasks. A *form letter* is one of the most common uses. This is a letter made up from a 'form' which looks like an original. Form letters are constructed from standard text paragraphs and have the address, name, date and any specific information inserted in the blank spaces. They can be used for routine correspondence, enquiries, confirmation and rejection letters. The fact that most offices have word processing available makes this a relatively simple process. It is certainly time saving.

To set up a series of form letters, collect some sample (outgoing) letters of the same kind and analyse them for common information. From these samples draft 'base' letters. First assign each a category heading ('Thank you', 'Enquiry', etc.) and then a letter of the alphabet. Number each paragraph. 'Mix and match' form letters can then be created through the use of standardised paragraphs. When instructing the word processing operator you merely indicate Letter A, para 4 or enquiry letter, paras 4 and 6.

The use of this system is not restricted to letters. Any document that is created regularly (sales reports, monthly statistics, etc.) is suitable for turning into a standardised form.

Forms can be any size, and frequently contain **checklists** or boxes to tick. To design your own forms you can work from existing documents or start from scratch. With existing papers, start by analysing them looking for common features, tasks or procedures which could be standardised. Without some documentation, walk yourself through a procedure or process listing each of the steps and then type up the list. Draw in some lines or boxes for filling in and make several photocopies. Test your model form for several weeks involving as many people as possible in the test. Make any modifications needed and when you are confident that it works, print your form.

It is worthwhile to establish a form file which contains samples of all the forms you produce. Label each form in the file and, if you wish, include a completed form to show an example of the responses.

Freedom trail

The more control you have over the timing and content of your job the higher your number on the freedom trail. The freedom trail is a continuum with a scale of five:

No. 1—you can't act until you are told what to do
No. 2—you need to ask what to do next
No. 3—you can act, but you need to tell your supervisor/manager as soon after you act as possible
No. 4—you can act, but you need to advise your supervisor/manager at your next regular meeting
No. 5—you can act entirely on your own

The two factors which most influence your point on the trail are your boss's ability to delegate and your own knowledge and skill on the job. Waiting to be told or not having the freedom to act on your own greatly restricts your time. Check to see that you are showing enough initiative and that you are meeting deadlines. Then work your way carefully up the freedom trail. (See also **Delegation**.)

G

Gantt charts

Charts used to plan and monitor activities. They were designed by Henry Gantt who worked for the US government during World War II. They have been described as 'horizontal time-tables or timelines' and consist of a series of rows or horizontal columns each allocated to a particular step, activity or task. They can show starting dates, deadlines and responsibilities (see figure 8).

Gantt charts can help considerably with **planning**, as they enable you to see at a glance the stage of a project and the amount of time needed to complete the job. Gantt charts are often colour coded for easier reference. Almost any computer software program for project management will include the format for a Gantt chart.

Goal calendar

A sheet of paper divided into sections, each section representing a period of time required to reach your goal. A large piece of paper with lots of colour and even pictures to act as prompts which you can hang on a wall works well. But a small calendar which fits into your **diary** will do—providing you check it daily (see figure 9).

For left-brain dominant people (see **Brain dominance**), the sections could be equal-size boxes. For the right-brain dominant, the petals of a flower or a series of intersecting circles might be better. Whatever method you use, each segment should contain a date and a step or target you plan to achieve during that time period. For a long-range goal, your segments might be months; for a shorter term goal, weeks or days. What you are doing is using this as a reminder device to help you

Figure 8   Gantt chart

CONFERENCE PLANNER

Committee:

Chairperson:

WHAT	WHO	WHEN	

see the steps clearly and to give you a sense of achievement as you complete each step.

Figure 9   Six-month goal calendar

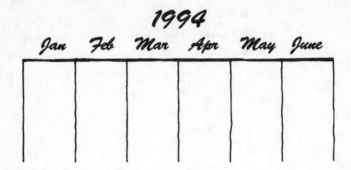

Goals

Things you want to achieve, targets of your behaviour, dreams. Next to **procrastination** (closely linked to a lack of goal setting), more words have probably been written about goals than any other topic in time management. Books have been devoted to the subject! It is generally agreed that the setting of goals is a crucial part of constructive time management. Ten basic guidelines follow:

1   Identify what you want and be *specific*. This means being absolutely clear about what you want to achieve. 'Meet deadlines for reports' is not a specific goal. 'Finish first draft of sales report with all figures correct by Friday, 14 August' *is* a specific goal. Don't restrict yourself to work or professional goals. Personal/life goals are just as (more?) important and help to keep you in balance.

2   To make a goal strong and to make it measurable, it is necessary to *set timetables*. Your time horizons can be short, medium or long term (give these timeframes your own meaning as definitions vary—'short' for some people is one day, for others six months).

3   Estimate how much time you need to complete each goal *by working backwards*. Start with the target date and list in reverse order all the tasks that need to be completed.

Working backwards seems to force home the reality of timelines.

4   Write or key in or chart or draw or journalise your goals. Find some way to record them in a medium that works for you. Try using coloured pens, coloured paper, **index cards**. The important thing is to *register* them.

5   Check your goals against your *values*. If your goals are not in harmony with your personal values you will feel constant emotional pressure as you attempt to achieve something in which you do not believe. This pressure may not just slow you down but cause you to actively sabotage your own goals.

6   Set some *priorities*. Often we seem to have too many goals without taking the care to determine what is really important. Being busy is not the key to successful time management. It is working on the right goal, at the right time, in the right way. Measure each of your goals against the others to try to determine those which will make a significant difference in what you want to achieve.

7   Check your goals against your *resources*. It's all very well to have a goal to revamp your organisation's computer system, but if your budget won't take the strain then that goal merely becomes a cause of anger and frustration. People, time and money are all resources which need to be checked.

8   Build in a *reward* system. There should be some 'prize' for successfully achieving your goals. If completing an MBA was one of your long-term goals, the framed degree at the end may be sufficient reward . . . or perhaps it's that overseas holiday you've been promising your family during the years they put up with your short temper and long hours.

9   Take some *action* daily to move you towards your goals. Remember **elephant eating**. Taking small bites enables you to shift yourself closer and closer to the end goal.

10 Be certain to *regularly review* your goals. As time passes, values and **priorities** change. As these change, so should your goals. Make your own definition of 'regularly'. For some people that's a daily review, for others weekly or monthly. The significant point is to change with the times, not sit on outdated and outmoded goals.

Frequently you may be working with team goals and/or

organisational goals. The *principles* of goal setting are the same. The difference is the need for agreement amongst everyone involved in the accomplishment of the goal about the *process* of setting and reaching it, as well as the goal itself.

Gonnas

People who suffer from a chronic complaint. They are forever making promises to *themselves* which are rarely, if ever, kept. Excessive **procrastination** and/or disorganisation keep them impotent.

Gonnas say things like: 'I'm gonna get a better job' or 'Someday I'm gonna save enough to travel' or 'Soon I'm gonna quit smoking' or 'I'm gonna do that planning soon'.

A close relative of the 'Gonna' is the 'Can do'. These are the people who make promises to *others* which are rarely, if ever, kept. The 'Can do' agrees to (or suggests) impossible deadlines, often fails to deliver, and follows through only when closely supervised. More time is spent trying to look as if they are doing something than actually doing it. When they fail to deliver they blame it on bad luck or someone else.

If either of these characters sounds like you, stop procrastinating and start acting. Set firm start-up times for yourself and follow some anti-procrastination guidelines. Be wary of volunteering for work which is beyond your time capacity. If you have a 'Gonna' or a 'Can do' working for you, be firm in rejecting promises you don't believe they will keep. When assigning work, be specific about expectations and deadlines.

Talk through potential roadblocks and bring all the issues out into the open. Give plenty of praise when **deadlines** are met as this helps reinforce acceptable time management.

Green light time

Mind freedom during personal **brainstorming**. When you are searching for an idea, keep the green light on all the time. Nothing should be done to stop the flow of thoughts. No evaluation. No interference. Just ideas. Once you have exhausted the flow, then you can begin to look critically at what is possible.

Green light time can also refer to that time in which you make yourself available to team members and colleagues. Get some signals arranged with others to indicate when your time is 'green' and when it is 'red' (not free). Hand signals, signs on your door, **answering machine** on . . . whatever will give the message about your availability.

Grouping

Gathering similar tasks and responsibilities and completing them together. There is an assumption that each time you complete a task you will become faster and better at doing it. If you have several letters to write, accounts to pay, journal articles to read, put them together into one time block and complete the group.

This is one of the more obvious of time management 'tricks' and yet one of the least followed. Right-brain dominant people (see **Brain dominance**) get excitement by always doing new things and they need to practise strong self control to 'group'. Anything that requires the same routines, forms, mental processes, location, equipment or even reference material can be grouped. If some of your like tasks occur regularly (daily, weekly, monthly), block out a standard time period for them on your calendar and get into the habit of grouping. (See also **Consolidation**.)

G.U.T.S.

A desk-clearing formula devised by US educator Charles Riley. Riley suggests that as you work to get rid of the junk which has accumulated on your desk you follow the G.U.T.S. formula. Each time you pick up an item, decide to act and either G=give it away, U=use it, T=throw it away or S=sell it. Based on some of the desks around, that last activity might be a money-making proposition.

H

Habit

The performance of a certain action *below our level of awareness.*
Forming the right habits is one of the keys to becoming a
successful time manager. When we execute a habit, something
cues our behaviour and we react to that cue. Changing a habit
means bringing the action into our level of awareness, changing the action which responds to the cue, and then making
the change so ingrained that we still behave in the new way
even when the action is below our level of awareness again.

How do you change a habit? Here are some basic guidelines. They look simple. Do not be deceived.

1 Identify the habit you want to change.
2 Decide what you want the new habit to be like and set the
   rules for that behaviour.
3 Identify the cue(s).
4 Act as soon as the opportunity arises.
5 Start as strongly as possible.
6 Consciously associate the cue(s) with the behaviour.
7 Do not allow *any* exceptions or deviations from your new
   practice.
8 Practise the new behaviour, preferably at the same time, in
   the same way, as often as possible.

You can *mentally* practise your new habit without actually doing
it. The best time for this is when the brain waves are in an
alpha (relaxed) state. This is usually just as you wake up in
the morning or before you fall asleep at night. To practise, lie
quietly with your eyes closed, breathe deeply and visualise
yourself performing the new habit. One or two minutes a day
of this practice will help reinforce the behaviour. Of course
you have to get into the habit of doing it. . .

Hidden time

Time previously wasted or not used productively. You probably have more hidden time each day than you realise. To help identify it, do a **time log** for a day or two. Make the log detailed so you can pick out the hidden periods. Hidden time is usually in minutes not hours.

How many productive things can you do in 5 minutes? Keep your list of 5-minute tasks handy and do some in your hidden time. Feel free to spend some hidden time doing 'nothing' (daydreaming, relaxing). This is an excellent means of **stress** reduction. It can also end up being very productive as some of our best ideas come when we are relaxed.

Hierarchy of wasted effort

A multiplier effect which happens when ineffective **delegation** filters down through the organisation hierarchy. You can be good at delegating, but what if what you delegate is out of alignment with organisational **priorities**? All you will do is compound ineffectiveness and waste the effort of the person to whom you delegate.

'To avoid delegating for ineffectiveness', Dale McConkey in *No-Nonsense Delegation* suggests that 'managers must first make basic decisions with respect to what really needs to be done and what the relative priority of each major objective that needs to be achieved is'. You will also need to work at 'what doesn't need to be done' and make certain that it is eliminated—not delegated. Be clear about the **objectives** and priorities of the whole enterprise. Then aim your delegations towards that end. Constantly question whether what you are asking your team members to do will help to further those objectives.

Homework habit

The bad and frustrating habit of taking work home from the office. Break this habit as quickly as possible. Refuse to take work home without asking yourself honestly why you cannot organise your workday sufficiently so that the necessary tasks can be completed.

Think carefully about your **delegation** skills. Are you taking other people's work home to 'polish it off'? This is excellent training for team members who quickly learn that it doesn't matter whether they do a good job or not because the boss will 'take it home and fix it'.

If you absolutely, positively, definitely have to take work home:

1 Do it only in response to a *very* tight deadline. These deadlines should not be regular occurrences. If they are, go back to the **planning** board.
2 Limit the type of work you are prepared to take home. This also controls the number of briefcases you need to pack before you leave the office.
3 Do some exercise or practise relaxation strategies before you plunge into the work.
4 Limit the amount of time you are prepared to spend on your task. You are likely to finish within that timeframe.

Hook

A way to end a telephone conversation that has gone on too long. At the very beginning of the conversation try to find out *what the person was doing when you called* (e.g. drafting a letter). Be subtle in your questioning but you won't find it hard to pick up a clue.

Once you have your 'hook', make a quick note about it on your pad so you won't forget. Then, when you want to end the conversation, tell the person that you know they want to get back to drafting that letter or whatever it was (the hook) and politely end the call. (See also **Interruptions** and **Telephone**.)

Household time management

Pretend you are running a small office, and apply the same principles of time management to your home. The ideas and concepts apply equally well for organising housework, cupboards and closets, clothes and accessories, **telephone** calls, drop-in visitors and children. A good paper management system is essential.

I

Ideas notebook

The place where you record all those good ideas, reminders, speculations. Use a pocket- or purse-size notebook or a mini tape recorder. Carry it with you everywhere and jot down whatever comes to mind. It doesn't matter how much you discard later, what is important it that you capture your thoughts. To help stimulate staff, you might like to key in one of your ideas and circulate it via **electronic mail** for comment.

Indecision

Vacillation, hesitation, dithering—anything rather than deciding. If you suffer from this disease it may be because you have a strong desire for perfection or a heightened fear of being wrong.

If you find yourself always needing more information, more computer printouts, more meetings, stop and ask yourself, 'Is any of this really going to improve the quality of the decision I need to make'? It may help to list on paper those obstacles which seem to be blocking your decision making. When the list gets too long, have a good laugh at yourself and then DECIDE! (See also **Decision Making**.)

Index cards

The 3 x 5 inch cards (apologies to metric fanatics) which proficient time managers are never without. Keep at least six in your pocket or purse or inside the flap of your diary. The advantage of using cards is that the information recorded can be moved around until the order you want is achieved: notes for a speech, **priorities** for a meeting, information to be transferred to your **diary**, trying out a new organisation chart. Use a bunch of index cards clipped or rubber-banded for your **ideas notebook**.

Information search

A way of getting more data. Although we all suffer from information overload, there are times when you *do* need more information. Data are used for many purposes including corporate, promotion, product, price, marketing, distribution and customer-service planning. If the information you need is not coming across your desk you may need to do some research on an 'ad hoc' basis.

Much of the information that you need for **decision making** may be produced in the normal course of running the organisation. Find out how to tap into those resources. Other information is available from 'off the peg' published sources (directories, year books, government statistics), through syndicated on-line data bases or from special information services such as the Australian Bureau of Statistics or the United States Consulate Information Service.

To speed your information search, start by describing in detail exactly what information you want and why you want it. Ask yourself what results you want to achieve. Then list the type of data you believe will help and work your way through these steps until you find what you want:

1 Talk with your internal sources, e.g. head of computing, company librarian. If you are lucky they may take over the information search for you. (**Delegation**, delegation, delegation!)
2 Talk with external sources, e.g. community or university librarians, other corporate librarians.
3 Look through indexes of books, periodicals, newspapers.
4 Consult indexes of government publications.
5 Consult directories of on-line, computerised data bases.

Interruptions

One of the biggest blocks to successful time management.

They need to be prevented or reduced. Dealing with interruptions is a 'no-win' situation. You are constantly trying to maintain that half-open door, looking for a balance between your need to be available to staff (open door) and the need for freedom from interruptions (closed door) to concentrate on high priority tasks. **Planning** is one of the keys to interruption prevention. The more you can anticipate problems, delegate and train, the fewer will be your interruptions.

Log: Start by taking a **time log** of all interruptions for one week. Record the time the interruptions occur, how long they take, who's involved, what the interruption is about, and how important it is. Then analyse them looking for patterns. For example, are the same people causing most of the interruptions? Are you receiving the same type of interruptions over and over again? Once you have this information you can design some prevention strategies. (See also **D & I chart**.)

Openings and closings: Interruptions have three distinct phases. Phase one is preliminary socialising, phase two is the reason for the interruption and phase three is the closing socialising. Often the socialising takes more time than the reason for the interruption. So practise good openings and closings and have some interruption-beating phrases handy such as:

- 'I'm busy now but I'll get back to you when I finish.'
- 'Let's settle this quickly so I can get back to that report.'
- 'Before we finish. . .'

Basic strategies

1 Practice MBWA (management by wandering around); the more you go out to meet staff and deal with their problems on the spot, the less they will need to come and interrupt you.
2 Check that your **follow-up systems** are working.
3 Schedule routine meetings with staff to check **priorities**.
4 Ask everyone to bring at least two possible solutions with every problem (once they have thought this through they may just solve the problem without interrupting you).
5 If your boss is the major interrupter, schedule a short daily meeting in the morning to align priorities.
6 Set fixed times each day when you are running 'open house'.

7   Set fixed times each day when your door is closed.

If you can't avoid the interruption, scribble yourself a quick note to show you where you were before you were interrupted. This will make it easier to get back on track when your visitor leaves.

One very common type of interruption which causes endless frustration is **telephone** calls that come during a meeting with your boss in his or her office. Try arranging the meeting in a conference room or in *your* office. Try asking that calls be held until your discussion is finished. When all else fails:

1   Use your waiting time to analyse the discussion you have been having and to modify your approach if necessary.
2   Be prepared to quickly recap the discussion thus far.
3   Prepare a list of the key points of your subject prior to your meeting. If time prevented a full discussion, you can leave the list with your boss when you leave.
4   Recognise that your boss may like the interruption as it gives a sense of power. Decide whether you are prepared to play this power game.

Try hanging some of the 'signs of interruption' (figure 5) on your door, or on the corner of your desk if you have no door.

If you are the one doing the interrupting, try this. Set up a file folder for each person who reports to you. In each folder, accumulate items to bring up at a fixed meeting time. Then think twice before you leap up and interrupt someone. (See also **Drop-in visitors**.)

Itinerary

A good, detailed list of travel information. It can be an invaluable time saver. Your itinerary should contain:

1   Arrival, departure and check-in times for all points on the trip expressed in local time and using the 24-hour clock.
2   Accommodation arrangements including the name, address and contact number, check-in and check-out times.
3   Time, name, address and contact number for all **appointments**.
4   Reminders such as rental car details.

Get the itinerary prepared on heavy paper as it will be folded and referred to many times during the trip. Have at least four copies prepared:

1 Two copies for you (put in two different places).
2 Copy for the file.
3 Copy to contact person in the organisation.

J

Job function analysis

A process designed to show you the gaps between your job **objectives** and what you actually do. Merrill and Donna Douglass in *Manage Your Time, Manage Your Work, Manage Yourself* suggest that you start your analysis by writing a short outline of what your job contains, breaking each section down into meaningful parts. Then you can 'view your job from three different perspectives: (1) what you think you are doing, (2) what you ought to be doing, and (3) what you are actually doing'.

To simplify the interpretation, the Douglass's suggest ruling a page into five columns with headings as shown in figure 10. The last three columns should each total 100 per cent. Don't overload the worksheet with detail, but complete it sufficiently to show the differences between estimated and actual time spent on each objective. Once you have seen the discrepancies, you can decide how to make adjustments in your time management to more closely align your key objectives with the tasks you undertake.

Figure 10   Job function analysis worksheet

Job function	Priority value	Estimated time %	Ideal time %	Actual time %

Journal

A form of writing that allows total freedom of expression. Keeping a daily journal or personal **diary** can help change your time management behaviour. A journal is private. There are no rules about what you write or the style in which you write it. It is merely a tool which provides you with the means to review the past and to look at how you might deal with the future. The more frequently you write up your journal the more often you take time to reflect.

For your journal select a writing book which makes you feel good, and which has plenty of space for you to write (or draw) what you wish. Write regularly, write fast, write everything and anything you wish. You can start with the immediate or go back to the beginning of the day and explore your thoughts, feelings, interactions.

When the time feels right, re-read what you have written. You may then begin to make some time management connections. For example, you may find that you procrastinate each time you are required to perform a certain task. Once you have made this connection you can begin to practise some anti-**procrastination** strategies.

Joy break

A relaxing and refreshing fun break that can take less than 5 minutes. Ann McGee-Cooper in *Time Management for Unmanageable People* suggests that you consider: 'What's fun for you? What do you like to do best? What gives you joy?'. McGee-Cooper feels that adults often lose their capacity for unstructured, non-competitive fun. This deprives them of a way to revive their energy. She suggests that you make a list of 'things that are fun for you and then divide them into four categories: 2–5 minutes, 5–30 minutes, 30 minutes to half a day, and half a day or longer'.

Once you have your list, use it to guide you as you build some regular joy breaks into your life.

K

Key results areas

The main areas and central elements into which work and personal life can be divided. Key results areas (KRAs) are the key outputs, the critical elements, that your position delivers. They are the areas on which you have to concentrate to achieve your goals and create results.

To develop a workable set of KRAs, you need to consider:

1 Your personal **mission statement**.
2 Your organisation's mission statement.
3 Daily influences, both internal and external.
4 Any desired changes in performance—your own and your teams.
5 A summary of your **time logs**.

Once you have gathered this information, and anything else which might help you to think through what you want to achieve, you can starting writing your KRAs. Keep the number manageable—seven to nine. In their publication *Key Areas*, Time Manager International suggest that you start by listing 'all your daily activities as they come to mind'. Then put them in **categories** (key areas) grouping them logically and 'give each group a heading'. After the KRAs have been identified, you need to translate them into **goals** and actions. At this stage you must be specific about who is going to do what, when and how, using what resources. Then follow your usual **planning** procedure using your daily **'to do' list** or other device to help you follow through and deliver the results.

If you wish, you can purchase **planners** with specific sections designed to help you to organise your time using KRAs as the base.

Kitchen message centre

When messages are getting out of hand, and family members are not doing their chores, this can help. Draw a chart with a section heading for each family member. Put all messages, notes and reminders under the name of the person involved. This system works equally well in an office or factory. The main thing you need to do is to train the people involved to refer to the message centre regularly.

L

Last job leftovers

Tasks which have *not* been left behind when someone changes jobs. People take their leftovers away with them because they like doing them. It makes them 'feel good'. Last job leftovers are time eaters. They also create resentment towards you from your replacement. After all, aren't these tasks their responsibility?

To shed this habit, check through your tasks carefully. Be ruthless about returning to its owner anything that you have carried with you. At the same time, you might like to check for another form of leftovers. These are tasks you inherit with your new position. These 'dead' tasks are still being completed because 'we've always done it that way' or 'the previous person who held this job liked to do that'.

Leading task

The term applied to a task that is helping you to start . . . to begin . . . to commence . . . to embark on a high priority assignment. While you may not feel up to doing the whole job right away, completing a leading task, such as collecting all the papers necessary to start working on next year's budget, may help to propel you towards your target.

Leisure time

Something you will have more of if you practise good time management. **Workaholics** excepted. It is the last thing they want!

Limited targeting

A way of limiting effort to one specific goal at a time, rather than aiming for six things at once. With practice you will be able to focus on that target only and not dissipate your energy. To limit your targets, apply some basic action-planning rules. Know your target, know how you will measure it, create a plan, break it into small action steps and follow your plan.

Lists

A way of recording and classifying information. When in doubt, *write* it out! But don't be like a friend who said she was now organised because she had made a list of her lists. Some people say they can keep their lists in their head. They usually tell you this just before frantically trying to remember something else they wanted to tell you!

Low payoff activities

Tasks which will make little, if any, impact on your key **goals**. Sometimes deciding *not* to do a task can be your most meaningful choice of the day. The point is that if you devote time to something with a low payoff, chances are that something with a higher payoff is being neglected. Part of the problem may be your inability to take risks. Working on low payoff tasks usually means doing something that feels comfortable and is relatively easy.

To get yourself focused on high payoff activities, start by reviewing your **delegation** strategies. Low payoff tasks are ones which are often the easiest to give to someone else to do. Look at swapping tasks and negotiating rosters for sharing of things such as **telephone** answering. If you must do low payoff activities, group similar tasks and systematise the work wherever possible. And don't worry about the standard. A low payoff task usually needs to be done only to minimum quality. Always ask yourself what will happen if the activity does not get done at all. Sometimes not doing something is the best use of your time.

M

Macro time managers

People who focus on tasks which will make a significant contribution to the organisation. William Brooks and Terry Mullins in *High Impact Time Management* say that macro time managers 'understand that determining what *not* to do is their most important task'. They 'refuse to become involved in low-impact projects'.

Macro time managers always set **priorities** and evaluate risks and know that doing the right thing is more important than doing the thing right.

Mail

Something you should try to find someone else to open and sort for you. Given some general guidelines, they will be far more ruthless with junk mail and re-direction than you would be.

Whether you delegate sorting or not, you need a good system. Start by getting some 3 x 5 **index cards** or cut some old paper into 7.5 x 12.5 cm strips. As you sort through your mail each day place the items in broad categories, e.g. urgent, reports, action today, follow up—whatever seems to work for you. At the end of each sort, write the name of the category on a card. Do this for three or four days until a pattern emerges. Then go through the **categories** and see what you can merge.

Once you have settled on the categories, decide the medium you will use for sorting. Manila folders work well. Label them and find a good, easy-to-reach place to file them. If possible, train an assistant to not only sort your mail but to deal with everything (including responses to correspondence) except that which you absolutely must see. If this makes you nervous, ask the assistant to prepare a mail summary letting you know what came in and how it was dealt with. Once trust develops, you will be able to discard the summary.

Mañana principle

A form of **procrastination** which enables you to practise self-deception. Why do today what you can put off until tomorrow (mañana)? Tomorrow you may have the inspiration, the motivation, the excitement, the right tools, be more rested. To overcome mañana, check for patterns and diversions. Then use some anti-procrastination techniques.

Master list

A way of listing everything you need to do in one place. A master list has no **priorities**. It is just a running, continuous list. Keep it in a small notebook which fits easily into your purse or pocket, or use a mini-recorder. Add items wherever and whenever you need to remember something. Then, when you are creating your daily '**to do' list** and setting up **diary** dates, take out your master list and use it to help jog your memory and guide your **planning**.

MBE (management by exception)

A way of managing or **delegation** which allows the maximum freedom for a team member. Once the task/problem/decision has been delegated (together with the appropriate authority and responsibility), the manager does not supervise the team member and only gets involved 'by exception'. This happens when something unusual or undesirable occurs or when the performance of the team member falls below an acceptable level. (See also **Delegation**.)

Measles method

A method used to help you to spot (sic!) excessive, repetitive

paperwork. Have a pencil handy. As you open your mail or work through your daily files, put a dot in the corner of each piece of paper. The next time you sort through add another dot. When your papers start to break out in measles it's time to look at some effective paperwork management strategies.

Meetings

The activity during which we experience the largest quantity of unproductive time. Beware if meetings are satisfying one of your psychological needs such as the need to look important, get away from the desk, imagine you are a leader, catch up with gossip, have a nice morning tea at company expense, pretend that you are a participative manager.

Most teams fail to sort out their meeting problems because they don't take the time to discuss the meeting *process* (what people were thinking/feeling; how the meeting was conducted, etc.) and only consider the meeting *content* (the topics on the **agenda**). Establishing a sound **critique** process will help.

Before you go to a meeting consider:

1 Is it necessary?
2 Why are you attending?
3 Not going or 'forgetting' to go.
4 Limiting the time you are prepared to spend at it.
5 Sending a deputy and asking them to make notes.
6 Asking your boss to go instead.
7 Using **teleconferencing** or **videoconferencing**.
8 Computing the cost per minute (total salaries plus fringe benefits of each person attending—this doesn't include preparation time, agenda keyboarding, etc.) and tabling this at the meeting.
9 Cancelling a regular meeting occasionally to test the need for it.

To help speed the meeting process:

1 Choose an appropriate venue.
2 Circulate the objective of the meeting in advance.
3 Set a time limit for each agenda item and for the meeting and stick to it.
4 Start on time.

5 Don't wait for latecomers (and don't waste everyone else's time catching them up), or close and lock the door after the meeting has started.

6 Appoint a timekeeper.

7 Hold a stand-up meeting (Look, no chairs!).

8 Limit participation.

9 Control **interruptions**. Have a rule that nobody (the chairperson included) takes calls during the meeting.

10 Hold the meeting just before lunch or just before the end of the normal workday.

11 Put items of interest to habitual latecomers at the top of the agenda.

12 Reduce all meetings to half their normal time.

13 Have a supply of overhead projector transparencies available with blocks of time marked off; members put in crosses when they are unavailable; stack the transparencies and hold them up to the light to see immediately when everyone has a time available for the next meeting.

14 Critique/review the meeting *process*. Use a meeting evaluation checklist or a **meetings scorecard** as an occasional spot check.

15 Finish on time.

If you are the chairperson:

1 Agree on the critique process.

2 Quickly and briefly summarise disagreements and reconfirm points.

3 Involve the group in resolving conflict.

4 Protect the silent members and control the talkers.

5 Treat all suggestions seriously.

6 Handle disruptive behaviour immediately.

7 Use active listening.

8 Keep your temper in check.

9 Interrupt talkers with a question.

10 Don't embarrass anyone.

11 Check regularly for feelings of attendees.

12 Review decisions and conclusions to reinforce them.

13 Stick to the **agenda**.

14 Don't be overly democratic or too rigid.

15 Allow some people to leave if they have already made their contribution.

16 Suggest that the position of chairperson be rotated amongst the team.
17 End on time.

After the meeting:

1 Have the minutes circulated within 24 hours.
2 Establish a good **follow-up system**.
3 Critique the meeting.
4 Use a **meetings scorecard**.
5 Conduct regular committee audits and abolish **committees** which have outlived their usefulness. (See also **Committees**.)

If you are not chairing, control the time you spend at the meeting

1 At the right moment, gracefully ask if your presence is still required. If not, ask to be excused.
2 Sit at the back of the room and slip out when the meeting is no longer productive for you.
3 Open your **diary** and do some **planning**.
4 Do some serious thinking, keeping a mental note of what is being discussed.

When not to call a meeting:

1 When your mind is made up as to what to do.
2 When you 'feel it's being democratic'.
3 When the subject is not important.
4 When you know what should be done but don't want to take the responsibility.
5 When you are trying to outsmart the boss or a colleague.
6 When you need the meeting as the last chance to win a point.
7 When you have the urge for a power surge.

One last point. If you want your meetings to go faster, paint the meeting room red.

Meetings scorecard

A list of actions that participants think can make meetings more effective. Ask them to rate items after each meeting and discuss them briefly at the next meeting as part of your review. The list might include:

1 Did the right people attend?
2 Did the meeting run to schedule?
3 Did all participate equally and fairly?
4 How good was the chairing?
5 Was the **agenda** sent in advance?
6 Was the venue satisfactory?

Mind mapping

A right-brain technique (see **Brain dominance**) of drawing diagrams. Ron Cacioppe in *Mind Maps* describes it as 'a diagram constructed according to certain guidelines using words, lines, shapes, colours and pictures'. Mind mapping is a way of freeing up your mind from left-brain constraints, and capturing your key ideas. To draw a mind map all you need is a blank sheet of paper and something to write with. If you wish, use coloured pencils to add a different complexion to your work.

Start by putting your key idea in the centre of the page and work outwards, recording key words, phrases, images which relate to your key idea. Use lines, arrows, shapes, colours, shading, symbols—anything which helps to represent your idea (see figure 11). Once you start mind mapping you will develop your own style. You can use mind maps to plan, make notes, write your **'to do' list**, brainstorm an idea, prepare a presentation, draft a document.

Mission statement

A dynamic, living document that describes the essence of a business or other enterprise, its philosophy and the values under which it expects to operate. A *personal* mission statement can help to guide you so that your investments in time and **energy** are compatible with where you want to go. It is a statement about what you want to be and do, and the standards and values which will guide you in your mission. It is a positive statement and contains no tasks—only visions.

Figure 11 Mind map

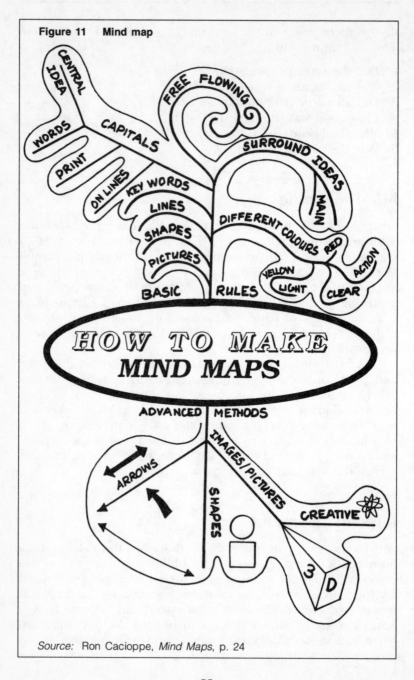

To prepare a personal mission statement, find a quiet place to work and start by writing an ending to these sentences:

1 The activities in my work life that I find most worthwhile are . . .
2 The activities in my personal life that I find most worthwhile are . . .
3 My basic purpose in business and in life is. . .
4 The essence of my current business or professional role is . . .
5 The way I feel about my current business or professional role is . . .
6 I bring these distinctive qualities to my current business or professional role . . .
7 The philosophical issues, personal values and **priorities** that are important to my business or professional future are . . .
8 What I would like to be able to do that I am not doing now is . . .
9 The thing I currently admire most about myself is. . .
10 What I would like to be different about my business or professional situation in 3 years is . . .

Once you have responded to these questions, and any others that you wish to add to your list, try to draft a personal mission statement. Limit the number of words but capture the spirit of your vision. Then put it away for a few days and let it rest. In a week or so look at it again, make any revisions and adopt it as your mission. You can then post it on your **planning wall**, put a copy in your **diary**, on your **desk**, or any place where you will be reminded about your mission.

Mobile phone

See **Telephone**.

Monkey

A term used to describe an imposed time management problem. It was first used in this way by William Oncken, Jr and Donald Wass in their *Harvard Business Review* article 'Management time: who's got the monkey?'. The symbolism comes from the 'monkey on my back' expression. Whoever has the next move, when dialogue between two parties ends, has the monkey.

Oncken and Wass say that 'for every monkey there are two people involved—one to supervise it and one to work it'. The most common monkey is usually team member imposed time, although monkeys leap in all directions—upwards, downwards, sideways. It is easy to pick up monkeys without realising it (although most of us are givers as well as picker-uppers) and it happens in all levels of an organisation. Monkeys which are not dealt with quickly may turn into gorillas.

Oncken and Wass suggest that to help eliminate team member imposed time you should 'feed monkeys face-to-face or by **telephone** (never by mail), and preferably by appointment only. If you are not going to feed them, shoot them. This helps to control the monkey population and prevents starvation'. Once you have *these* monkeys under control you will increase your discretionary time to enable you to deal more effectively with boss-imposed or system-imposed time.

Monochronic time

Time which can be measured externally in specific units—days, hours, minutes. It is objective 'clock time', the way the left-brain looks at time and the opposite of **Polychronic time**. If you want to know how long a machine will take to print 50 pages, and the manual says the machine prints at 10 pages a minute, the answer is straightforward and monochronic. Five minutes!

On the other hand, if you want to know how long it will take to train a team member, the answer is more complex. Most organisations try to place a value on work in monochronic terms whereas many of us do jobs which are not easily measured in specific units.

Motivation

Something which drives an individual to action of a particular type. A motivated person is someone who is prepared to take that action. There are almost as many motivational theorists trying to explain what does or doesn't 'drive' people as there are stars in the sky. Some of the most popular names include Maslow, known for the much used and abused 'hierarchy of needs', Hertzberg, famous for his 'motivators and hygiene factors', and McClelland, who has firm ideas on power and motivation. Other theories have been grouped into *normative* (Likert, Blake & Mouton, Argyris) and *contingency* (Fiedler, Hersey & Blanchard) categories.

One traditional concept says that there are only three things that really motivate people: fear, incentive and attitude. Fear is the 'push' motivator and incentive the 'pull' motivator. Fear motivates because of the consequences if we don't do something. Four things will create incentive (known as the four Ps): praise, prestige, promotion and pay cheque. Attitude is the most difficult to deal with, as this is driven by internally set goals.

So-called 'new age thinking' suggests that traditional methods of motivation are no longer valid, particularly fear or the 'stick', part of the 'carrot and stick' method of motivation. New-agers believe that the 'creative subconscious' must provide the drive and energy to motivate someone. Before anyone can change, their self-image must change first. If you are comfortable with your self-image, you won't be motivated to change and grow.

Lack of motivation has an obvious impact on time management. In the first instance it can cause severe **procrastination**. Even if the procrastination is overcome, work output tends to be slow and slovenly, and errors and calls for help from the boss also increase. All this impacts on the time management of both the team member and the supervisor.

To help keep high performers motivated, push continuous personal improvement by providing advanced training and setting high standards and challenging goals. Use your high performers to teach others. For poor performers, check **goals** and objectives which may need resetting, coach and counsel regularly, look for new challenges and check for **stress** management. Whatever the motivation, all team members need support and praise. Frequent use of 'thank you' and 'well done' can sometimes be the best motivator available.

There is a plethora of so-called motivational tapes available. Many people find them useful and you can listen to them

91

while showering, dressing or driving—a good example of **doubling up** to make the best use of your time.

Myths

Unproven assumptions that have become part of time management legend. Here are 18 favourites:

1 The higher the level at which a decision is made the better.
2 People procrastinate because they work better under pressure.
3 If you work faster, you will accomplish what you need to.
4 The harder you (busy people) work the more that gets done.
5 There is never enough time to accomplish what is really important.
6 The open door policy improves a manager's effectiveness in dealing with team members.
7 It is impossible to find a block of time to devote to important projects every day.
8 Given a busy schedule, it's impossible to work on the basis of **priorities**.
9 Delay improves the quality of decisions.
10 If there were more hours in the day, people would finish what they need to do.
11 At least 8 hours of sleep is needed at night to function properly.
12 It's better to do small tasks first and save the big ones for later in the day.
13 Managers who are the most active get the most done.
14 Wasting time does not cost very much.
15 A good manager is indispensable.
16 Efficiency equals effectiveness.
17 By doing it yourself tasks are handled better and faster.
18 Identifying problems is the easy part of problem solving.

N

Navy pretest

A way to test whether ideas are worth putting into practice. Check these ten points devised by the US Navy before you try something new:

1 Will the idea increase productivity or improve quality?
2 Will this be a more efficient way to utilise people?
3 Will this improve operations, maintenance, or construction?
4 If equipment needs to be purchased, will it be an improvement over the present equipment?
5 Will it improve safety?
6 Will it reduce waste?
7 Will it eliminate unnecessary work?
8 Will it reduce costs?
9 Will it improve present office methods?
10 Will it improve working conditions?

'No'

The single most effective time-saving word in the English language. Every request for your time needs to be compatible with your own **priorities** or those of your department or the organisation. Because of your need for politeness, or perhaps feelings of inner guilt, you may be reluctant to say 'no', or may be confusing 'yes' with teamwork. If saying 'no' is difficult for you, practise, practise, practise. Use creative **visualisation** or just repeat 'no' over and over again in front of a mirror. Count to ten before responding to a request.

Not every 'no' has to be justified. However, if you find it easier to provide a reason try to do so without too many details, but leave the other person's values intact. Try 'No, I couldn't produce the quality for you, but let me make a suggestion. . .' Offering other options often helps get you off the hook.

If someone puts you under strong pressure for a 'yes' you may have to be tough and say, 'No, that is not on my list of **priorities**'. This is almost always a conversation stopper. If all else fails, call 'time out'. Tell them you'll think about it. This is less assertive but gives you time to practise saying 'no' in front of your mirror once again.

'Not to do' list

A list of things best left undone. It includes:

1 Anything you can delegate.
2 Anything that someone else should be doing for themself.
3 All low priority tasks unless your number one tasks have been completed.
4 Anything that nobody will notice if it isn't done.
5 Anything that you said 'yes' to when you should have said 'no'.

Note approach

Making 'notes' to remind yourself of something. If **procrastination** is your problem, using the note approach can help. Write small notes and attach them to something to remind you about the task. Yellow Post-it slips serve admirably. Attach them to your **diary**, a file, a journal, a nearby wall. Language students use this approach for learning vocabulary and yoga teachers suggest it to help pupils remember to breathe deeply and regularly.

O

Objectives

A description of an output you plan to achieve at some given time in the future. **Goals**, **targeting**, **mission statement** and **objectives** are shades of the same idea.

Office time savers

Ways to save time when doing office clerical work. To do this systematically, look at each discrete job and identify the individual tasks which need to be done to successfully complete the job, e.g. write a report, complete a form. Then look at each task and ask:

1 Is it needed? (If not, stop doing it.)
2 Is it being done at the right time in the office cycle?
3 Is it being done in the right office?
4 Can it be simplified it without losing its effectiveness?
5 Can it be combined with something else?
6 Could an outside service do it better, faster, cheaper?
7 Can you computerise the process?

Once you have identified the options, select those with the highest payoffs and act.

On-time personality

A quality which allows you to get a headstart on the day. Mark McCormack, writing in *Entrepreneur*, suggests some rules:

1 'Speed up when running behind; if a meeting runs longer than expected, cut down on the next one to catch up'.
2 'Avoid rush hours' and schedule flights, drives and dining

at times when they are least popular; fly midday, arrive at work early.
3 'Allow time for things to go wrong' by budgeting a bit of extra time.
4 Be early rather than late; this makes the best impression.

Open-door policy

An idea with good intentions often misinterpreted by the overly enthusiastic manager. The original concept was suggested as a way to encourage inaccessible managers to be more available to staff. Rather than allow anyone to interrupt you whenever the mood strikes them, establish a routine for one-to-one meetings that is respected by your team and allows you to work for healthy chunks of time without interference. (See also **Interruptions** and **Drop-in visitors**.)

P

Pace of life

That which is speeding up year after year. Think about it—particularly in relation to the fax or your mobile phone. When you receive a fax the inclination is to react immediately—usually with another fax even if the matter is not particularly important and doesn't relate to one of your A **priorities**.

And what about the **mobile phone**? Once upon a time driving was seen as a quiet period away from the **telephone**. Now you get calls in the car, at the theatre, at **meetings**, even in the lift.

Does this vary from place to place? Psychologist Robert Levine, writing in *Psychology Today*, describes a study done in 35 United States cities sampling how fast the population walked, talked and worked. He found the fastest paced cities were Boston, Buffalo and New York, all in the northeast. (Scores obtained in a similar study of an urban population in Japan went off the high side of the chart.)

Check your own pace against Levine's observations. The fastest pedestrians covered 18 metres (60 feet) in about 11 seconds, which was three and a half seconds faster than the slowest walkers. This means that while the fastest walkers travelled 100 metres the slowest were walking only 75. The fastest talkers read at 3.9 syllables a second compared with 2.8. Levine also observed that type-A (fast-paced) cities attract **Type-A** personalities.

What all this probably proves is that the time pressures in some places are higher than in others and that fast-paced environments may be stressful to slow-paced (Type-B) people. Do *you* work in a type-A or type-B place, and what is your pace of life?

Paperwork

One of the biggest time management headaches. Two things make people dysfunctional in relation to paperwork: lack of clear **objectives** and lack of a system.

Clear objectives provide a guide to what to retain and what to throw away. As you work, you need to constantly ask yourself 'How do I plan to use this piece of paper?'. Your system tells you what to do with the piece of paper. There are three cardinal rules:

1　Decide what to keep.
2　Decide where to put it.
3　Handle each piece of paper once only.

Whether you are dealing with incoming or outgoing paper, it helps to know your paperwork **prime time** (early morning?, late afternoon?) as that is when you will move the paper quickly.

Find a formula that works for you. The ABC method is one of the most popular. Separate the paper into piles according to priority A, B or C. Then re-sort the B pile into either A or C and place the C pile in the **C-drawer** (out of sight, out of mind). Then action the A pile.

Stephanie Winston (1983) says that there are only four-and-a-half things you can do with a piece of paper. You can: throw it away, refer it, act on it, file it, or (the 'one-half') read it. She has devised an acronym to help: TRAF.

Think of 'TRAFfic'—paper flowing from one point to another. TRAF stands for *T–Toss* which means throw it away, *R–Refer* which means delegate or send it on, *A–Act* which means action it, and *F–File* which means file it away, permanently or in your follow-up folder.

To deal with the 'one-half', anything which requires more than 5 to 10 minutes reading (5 minutes is enough when you are in a 'sorting paperwork' frame of mind) should go into your reading box or file.

Two other catchy formulas which may help as reminders: the 'Four Ds' Approach: Delegate, Defer, Destroy and Do; and the 'What, When, Where' Approach: What is it? When is it used? Where should it go?

To ease your paperwork problems, encourage people to report face-to-face and trust them to report *exceptions only*.

Provide incentives for cutting paperwork. Cost your **reports** and **forms**, audit them regularly and offer rewards for each form or report that can be eliminated or combined.

Don't type it, write it. Reply to letters and memos by writing an answer on the bottom and photocopy for the record (if needed). Use 'Speedi Forms'. These are preprinted, 'multipak' forms on which you can write or type your message. There is a copy for you, a place for the respondent to put their reply and a copy for them to keep.

Prepare by preprinting:

1 Postcards ready for repetitive correspondence; leave a space to write a short message by hand.
2 Labels for standard and repetitive correspondence.
3 Envelopes with the names of anyone you regularly send material; batch it and send out at fixed intervals.
4 Adhesive labels listing standard enquiry information such as prices, terms, etc.

Create a set of ready labels for recurring mailings by typing names and addresses on mastersheets using adhesive labels and reproduce by photocopying as needed.

Use window envelopes. Retain copies of your best memos and letters. Modify them and keep a file of reply 'starters'. Keep a **paragraph book**. Before **filing** or circulating a copy of a letter, make a note of whether and when a reply is required. Also specify whether a copy is to be retained after the reply is received. Try **colour coding** your paperwork: e.g. green always means accounting, blue sales, pink purchases.

Paragraph book

A book of your best common paragraphs on subjects that occur regularly in your day-to-day writing. To start, go through previous correspondence and collect your best efforts. Group them into **categories** by subject unless you have a more practical classification. Then break them down into paragraphs, give each paragraph a number and collate them in a looseleaf binder.

Make notes on each page where necessary and give a copy to anyone who does keyboarding for you. Then when you write or dictate you need only indicate the number of your paragraph and any extra items you wish inserted. If you don't wish to create your own paragraph book, you can purchase one or buy a book of samples of correspondence and use that as your base material.

Pareto's principle

See **Eighty–twenty rule**.

Parking system

A method to help you keep your desk clear and avoid losing messages. Develop a parking system for everything that comes into your office, including personal items. This is particularly important for **telephone** messages. Have a spike file or a small box strategically placed and let your assistants and colleagues know about your system. This is one way of helping to ensure minimum loss and misplacement.

Pathfinders

People whose lives are complex models for lives truly worth living. The term comes from the book *Pathfinders* by Gail Sheehy. Pathfinders are people who, when faced with risk and uncertainty, turn to four coping devices. They:

1 Work more.
2 Depend on friends.
3 See humour in the situation.
4 Pray.

Not bad advice for time managers.

Perceptual conflict

A different view of **objectives** and **priorities** because of the way people perceive events. It usually results from a lack of dialogue between parties as to what is important and what should be done first. One remedy is for both boss and team member to *independently* write down a list of the team member's major responsibilities and the intended results of each. Team members need to look closely at what they think the boss expects. When the lists have been completed a meeting should be held, the lists compared, expectations clarified and conflicts resolved. (See also **Circle overlap.**)

Perfectionism

A trap which wastes time. Perfectionists either delay doing tasks because they don't have enough time to make them perfect, or they spent too much time doing something perfectly when OK would be sufficient. Perfectionists need to recognise that what is below average to them may be perfectly acceptable to someone else.

To help avoid the perfectionism pitfall, try this trick. Pretend you are a university academic about to give a lecture to students on the topic, 'Why people can't be perfect'. Write a one-page summary of your proposed lecture. Then adopt your own ideas.

Try to be clear about the standard required of any task before you attempt it. Always ask yourself, 'What is the least work I can do on this and still have it acceptable to others?'. Apply the **Eighty–twenty rule.** Deliberately make some of your work 'less perfect' and then show your 'errors' to a close friend for comment.

Perhaps list

A list of ideas which you may wish to put into action sometime in the future. It is not a list of goals or commitments but a way to capture insights by writing them in a small notebook or recording them on your 'perhaps' tape. This frees you from being diverted from your main task by the idea, and you can review and reflect upon it at another time.

PERT

This is an acronym for *Program Evaluation and Review Technique* which is a method of flowcharting which graphically portrays relationships between different activities. The technique was developed by the US Navy to monitor the Polaris project. Its most common use is to help visualise and keep track of projects. To produce a PERT chart:

1 Set your goal.
2 Set your deadline.
3 Break your goal down into subtasks or units.
4 List all the subtasks in sequence.
5 Construct a diagram showing each subtask in order of performance; tasks may be handled one at a time in sequence or there may be several tasks handled in parallel.

PERT charts are often combined with CPM, the *Critical Path Method*. This enables you to identify complex, overlapping schedules and find the critical (longest) path to the goal. To combine PERT with CPM, follow steps 1 to 4 above and then add the estimated time to complete each task under ordinary conditions. By adding the times of all the tasks that appear along each of the diagrammed paths, you will find the critical path. Then you can look for ways to shorten it.

Planner

A physical organisation system which enables you to put all key activities and tasks in one place and to see the arrangements you have made concerning **priorities**, people, information, space and physical objects. 'Planner' is sometimes used as a generic term to refer to a **diary** or **calendar**. A planner is much more than that.

There are many varieties of planner on the market. A standard portable planner would be in a ring-binder cover with open/close rings and separate sections for priority categories. Many looseleaf planners take a 'mix and match' approach, enabling you to devise your own systems using those sections relevant to your routine. Typical sections include daily, weekly, monthly, annual and event calendars; sections for **goal** setting and **delegation** planning, project planning, 'to do' lists, priorities, key result areas, reminder lists, expense records and **telephone** numbers and addresses.

Wall planners are charts that allow for large visual display.

These are particularly valuable if you work on projects or in teams where others need to be able to see and follow the plan.

You can make your own planner—size, shape, colour are not important. What is vital is having a tool with a system that works *for you*. A good planning system will take arrangements out of your head and order them in one place. Remember that planning needs change with time and with jobs. If filling out the planner becomes a burden, and your time management is not improving, you need to question whether you have the right planning tool.

Planning

Something we never seem to have enough time to do. This is usually because we are 'too busy', not good at it, or 'like to keep our options open'. Planning is a way of connecting the future with the present and provides a means of controlling what we do and the order in which we do it. Lack of planning sets up a cycle of time management failure. This is what happens: you are too busy to plan, so your days and weeks get out of control. Then you are too busy running around putting out fires to have time to plan.

Planning starts by establishing your **goal(s)** and seeing the link between what you do and those goals. Having done this, ask yourself these planning questions:

1 What has to be done? Consider assumptions and conditions.
2 Who is the person to do it? If it is not you, then delegate it and focus on results, not activity.
3 If you are to do it, where is the best place to do it?
4 When should it start and when should it finish?
5 How much time will it require?
6 What are the **priorities**? Consider short, medium and long term.
7 How will you review and control it?

Once you have explored these questions you can begin to develop alternatives and make decisions to record and implement your plan.

To help you plan effectively, start by getting into a planning routine. For a typical day it need not take more than 5 to 10 minutes to plan, but your routine needs to develop to the stage that starting the day without a plan makes you feel guilty.

The best times to plan are either just before you leave work (to plan the next day) or first thing in the morning (for the current day). There are pros and cons for each time. The day's pressure begins first thing in the morning and it's easy to get caught up in activity and find your planning time has disappeared or you have lost concentration. Late afternoon or early evening you may be too tired to do justice to your plan. Your **bio-rhythms** can be a factor.

Once you have devised your plan you can begin to schedule your commitments. Schedule loosely and work backwards. If you know that you want to leave work by 5 pm consider how much time each of the tasks in your plan will take, add them together, and that will tell you how much time to schedule and when to start so that you can get away 'on time'. (See also **Backwards planning**.)

Planning wall

A place to put up your personal plan of action—a space that's all your own. You can look at your planning wall at any time and see exactly how your plan is progressing. To save your plan from becoming lonely you can also hang your **calendar**, some notes, a flowchart or some pictures to help to remind you to work to your plan. Use plenty of colour on your wall to focus your attention even more.

Polychronic time

Time that you cannot measure in the usual way, e.g. minutes, hours, days. It is subjective based on inner experiences and the opposite of **monochronic time**. How long does it take a newly appointed manager to establish team spirit? That is an example of polychronic time.

People with a strong dominance of the right brain (see **Brain dominance**) tend to think and work in polychronic time which is a state of mind and attitude. Predicting how long something will take to complete makes them feel uncomfortable, and they are reluctant to commit to timelines because of this. What if you get a new idea? What if your intuition tells you to change course midstream? These concerns mean that it is difficult to measure things in precise times.

Preferred day assessment

A way of looking at what you do on certain days to allow for your personal preferences. Just as our **bio-rhythms** or **prime times** influence how we work during particular times of the day, so we may also have preferred days on which we like to do certain tasks.

For example, some people work harder at the beginning of the week than at the end. Some prefer to use Monday to handle administrivia and then leave the rest of the week clear for their priority work. Some people get **energy** on Friday in anticipation of the weekend. For some there are 10 to 12 productive hours of a working day, for others 5 or 6.

If you can plan and adapt your working week to allow for these preferred days, then your **productivity** is likely to be high. Not being able to accommodate your preferences could mean that you are working below your potential.

Presentation

Something which often takes a long time to formulate. To cut corners, have one of your team members ghost-write it or have them do the bulk of the presentation—and you come in at the end to do the summarising. This is great for ego and team building. Dictate the presentation and work from a draft, or dictate the barest outline and let someone fill in the gaps for you.

For 'instant' presentations, write the objective of your talk on an **index card** and use this as your introduction. Then write every idea you have which supports your objective on separate cards. Look for examples which illustrate each idea. Staple them back to back. Sort out the ideas and use your best four or five. Then arrange them in order.

Pricing your time

A pragmatic task to help identify the impact of time management on your life. It is also a valuable way to point out the cost of wasted time, for example at non-productive **meetings**. Merrill and Donna Douglass (1980) suggest you start with your own salary and allow 100 per cent for overheads and 40 per cent for 'fringe benefits'. Add to this the salaries of any support staff and 140 per cent for their overheads and fringe benefits. Divide the total by the number of hours you spend working on your **key results areas**.

Figure 12 shows an example for Helena, a middle manager.

Figure 12   Pricing your time

Helena's salary	$34 000
Plus 100 per cent for overheads	34 000
Plus 40 per cent for fringe benefits	13 600
Support salaries (one assistant)	23 500
Plus 140 per cent for overheads/fringes	32 900
TOTAL	$138 000

To calculate Helena's weekly time cost, divide $138 000 by 52—about $2654. If Helena spends only half of her work time, say 20 hours, on her key results areas, the hourly cost of these is $133 per hour.

Do this exercise for yourself. Even if you have no support staff you will be surprised at your cost per key results hour. Try to be honest about the amount of time you spend on really productive work. Next time you begin an activity ask yourself if, given your cost per hour, it is worth your time to do it.

Then do a similar exercise combining the salaries of people at one of your **meetings**. Estimate how much of the meeting time was productive and then work out its costs. Present your findings at the next meeting and see what happens.

Prime time

When you feel most alert and capable of creative thought and high **productivity**. Most of us are either fowls (morning people) or owls (night people). Fortunately, flexitime gives us some opportunity to use our prime time more effectively. This is when you should be scheduling high priority, high payoff tasks. If you don't already know your prime time, jog in place for 5 minutes early in the morning, in the middle of the morning, mid-afternoon and late afternoon. Do this on a non-working day. Whichever session leaves you feeling the most invigorated pinpoints your prime time.

Experts suggest that we also have an *internal* prime time when we are at our best concentrating deeply and working alone, and an *external* prime time when we are best working with people.

Principle of calculated neglect

A theory that says that it is better to devote the majority of your time to the people whose contributions will produce the best results. This is a variation on the **Eighty–twenty rule** or **Pareto's principle**. Your neglect is 'calculated'; that is, you work out who will contribute the most, and give time to the rest if you have it. Don't feel badly if you leave someone off your list because you are off someone's list also. The same principle can be applied to tasks substituting 'what' for 'who'.

Priorities

Subjectively established precedence. The setting of priorities is one of the most critical functions of time management. To set priorities appropriate to the situation, first consider your **goals**. Then devise a system with *criteria attached to each level* of priority. The criteria you define will help determine whether your system will work or not. Three levels are probably enough. You can apply the principles of the **triage** system used in times of war, or A/B/C, or 1/2/3, or critical/soon/anytime, or high/medium/low or green/yellow/red (see figure 13).

If you have problems with conflicting priorities, it may help to sort priorities *visually* by having a variety of unusual containers or baskets in which to put working documents or reminder notes. Red or other coloured stick-on flags grab attention and act as reminders, as do coloured folders or cards.

Cards can be particularly helpful for sorting priorities and,

Figure 13   Priority setting systems

Criteria	Triage system	Numbers	Letters	Colours	Words	Words
If not done within 24 hours, my job is at risk and I will probably lose the affection of someone I care about.	Needs immediate attention or operation.	1	A	green	critical	high
If not done within 7 days, my job is at risk and I will probably lose the affection of someone I care about.	Is injured but can wait for treatment.	2	B	yellow	soon	medium
This needs to be done sometime in the future.	Victim will likely die, don't treat.	3	C	red	anytime	low

if you wish to go upmarket, you can buy specially designed folders with slots in which to place your cards in sequence.

For a simple method, decide how many levels you would like and keep a bunch of **index cards** in each colour on your desk. For each of your tasks, assign a level/colour and write it quickly on a card. Then sort the cards in each level into priority order. Put a rubber band around them (or clip with a bulldog clip), put them in a prominent, easy access spot, and then start doing your first-level tasks. From time to time review the cards in your second and lower levels. You may wish to change the level or throw the card away.

Some priority principles to consider include:

1   Put it in writing.
2   Consider the demands of others but practise the **principle of calculated neglect**.

108

3 Set priorities a day ahead if at all possible.
4 Practise **consolidation**.
5 Look beyond the details but keep your perspective.
6 Make one criterion for priority setting how much you enjoy doing a task—but don't let that be the sole criterion.
7 Consider the minimum time each task will take but don't let that be the controlling factor; priority not time should be paramount.
8 Consider your long-term career **objectives** when setting priorities.
9 Revise your priorities regularly.

Some experts suggest that you work on your number one priority until it is finished. Others suggest you tackle the hard jobs first. Still others suggest that you limit the time on your number one priority to 45 minutes or an hour because of **energy** and concentration levels. Sydney Love (1981) suggests using the *division principle*. This means that if a set of tasks are of equal utility and all are of high priority, do each task to the threshold value and then divide the remainder of the available time among them. Threshold value is the minimum amount needing to be done on each task in order to change its priority.

Whatever priority system you use, always track your progress. Climb up in an imaginary helicopter, circle over your work area and ask yourself the classic time management question: 'What is the best use of my time right now?'. Depending on the answer, you may wish to readjust your priorities.

Problem solving

Creating change to bring *actual* conditions closer to conditions that are *desired*. A problem can be any situation where things are not as they should be or as we wish them to be. The term 'problem solving' is often used interchangeably with **decision making**. Decision making is part of the problem solving process as, in order to solve the problem, it is necessary to decide what needs to be done and then to do it. Problem finding or problem analysis makes up the other part of problem solving.

Solving the *right problem* is often the problem. This means asking the right questions of the right people to find out what will most improve a troublesome situation, and recognising that problems have many causes, not just one. Ask yourself and/or your team:

1 What exactly is happening?
2 Who is involved?
3 What are the elements of the problem?
4 When does it happen?
5 Where does it happen?

The right problem is one in which all the 'stakeholders' agree that something is wrong and want to try to correct it. The result should have a positive effect or at least neutralise a negative situation.

As well as recognising the right problem, a good problem solver needs to anticipate developing problems and step in before they create too much trouble. You also need the communication skills to enable you to clearly state the problem and to work with the group or individual to get the information you need on which to base your decision.

There are many models with suggested steps for problem solving. Try this formula:

1 Assess the situation, gathering information and talking to stakeholders.
2 Identify and define the problem, stating it clearly.
3 Diagnose how big it is and what caused it.
4 Define your end goal.
5 Generate creative solutions for solving it: can you modify, minimise, substitute, rearrange, reverse or combine?
6 Decide the most desirable option.
7 Forecast potential problems.
8 Write a plan for implementation.
9 Build consensus and implement the plan.
10 Evaluate the success of strategies used.

Although it can be time consuming, it is better to take the time initially to identify the right problem and the right solution(s) rather than trying shortcuts. Otherwise you risk spending an inordinate amount of time clearing up the wrong solution to the wrong problem. In the meantime the 'right' problem will probably have become worse.

Procrastination

Delaying, deferring, putting off something that needs to be done. The consequences can affect you internally or externally, and the impact can be serious or mild. If you have been procrastinating over a major project, the **stress** of not doing it may cause your health to break down (internal and serious) or your boss may give you a poor performance rating (external and serious). If you have been wanting to reorganise your desk, you may feel badly about it (internal and mild) but the result is that your desk continues to look untidy (external and mild). There are many reasons that people procrastinate. These include:

1 Feeling overwhelmed because a single task seems unmanageable or feeling overburdened with an enormous list of tasks.
2 Fearing failure because of lack of skill, experience and knowledge and being judged on your performance.
3 Fearing success because if you reach the goal the 'prize' may be more hard work.
4 Seeking perfection not knowing how to achieve it in the time available.
5 The task is boring.
6 Fearing loss of autonomy and control because you want to do things when you are ready, not when someone else wants you to do them; you want your own rules.
7 The project may have a high payoff but be high risk.
8 The task is inherently unpleasant.
9 Something is important but not urgent.
10 Your self-esteem is low.
11 Failing to understand responsibilities.
12 You lack discipline.
13 Having an overly large workload.

Procrastinators commonly play games with themselves as excuses for the delay. One of the most popular is called 'When'. To play 'When' you justify your delay by saying that you will do something *when*. . .

* the time is right
* I'm not so busy
* I'm inspired

111

- I have the right computer program
- I can do it perfectly
- I've had some exercise
- I have more information
- things aren't so hectic

Procrastination is a bad **habit**. Like any habit you need to decide that you want to change and then practise the change until it becomes a new good habit. It may help you start if you can identify the reason(s) why you procrastinate. Use a procrastination notebook. Each time you sense you are procrastinating, jot down your reasons by getting yourself to respond to the questions *what*, *where*, *when*, *why* and *how*. Keep track of all the games and excuses you use, categorise them and look for patterns.

Pay attention to what you are thinking when you put things off. What are the excuses? What are you doing or feeling? Then pick a problem area you want to work on. Focus on one aspect of that activity and do it until it is under control. Once you have been successful (broken the habit) you can attempt another small part. Try to check out your feelings, asking, 'What is the worst thing that will happen if I do this job?'.

There are many 'tricks' that seem to work to help break the inertia of procrastination. Try some of these:

1 Consider the 'worst first' rather than 'worst last' approach—take your cod liver oil and then enjoy your ice cream for dessert rather than the other way around.
2 Set small deadlines and reward yourself when they are met.
3 Take 'baby steps' by breaking a job into small bits and pieces, making it more manageable; make a list on paper of each step; try making six phone calls instead of twelve or writing a first very rough draft rather than trying to finish the entire document; remember that you don't have to start at the beginning, you just have to start.
4 Use visible reminders—stick-on notes, signs, red 'flags'.
5 Set mini-competitions with yourself to see how quickly you can finish something.
6 Agree to work on something for only 4 minutes—this often gets you started and if you stop after 4 minutes at least you have completed that much of your task.
7 Share the burden by involving others in your activity—

going public sometimes helps keep you up to the mark especially if you promise someone else that the task will be done by a specific time; for a variation use a tape recorder and talk about your procrastination concerns.

8 Try saying, 'As long as I. . .' For example: 'As long as I have the budget file open I might as well look at last year's figures'.

9 Use the balance sheet method: on the left side of a piece of paper list the reasons for procrastination and on the right side the benefits of getting it done; compare your lists and confront your excuses.

10 Give yourself a penalty by agreeing to give up something you like if you don't start your task by a certain time.

There is such a thing as prudent postponement (purposeful procrastination). This is when you really do need more information, when it may well be valuable to wait and see, or when you need a change of pace or a little break. . . Under those circumstances it may be valuable to procrastinate—but not for too long. Accept this as a deliberate delay, rather than just more procrastination, and allow yourself to feel OK about it. Remember that 'a body in motion tends to stay in motion'. Once you start on a task, keep at it while your **energy** is up and try to schedule your important tasks into your **prime time**.

Staff procrastinators

If you have a procrastinator on your team, you have a responsibility to encourage them to make the best use of their time. Some of these suggestions may work:

1 When assigning work, set definite concrete steps and help them plan their schedule step by step; tell them what information is needed, how much, what is important; use numbers where possible.

2 Break an assignment into pieces; this allows the team member to isolate specific parts not understood and to ask for help.

3 Limit the number of assignments they are involved in at any one time.

113

4 Give the team member an office or work space that is as free of distractions as possible.

5 Watch the procrastinator's work habits; make gentle suggestions about changing behaviour.

6 Confront missed deadlines and poor performance directly; focus on results not on personalities.

7 Set up timelines and make them visible; mark intermediate deadlines and follow through.

8 Be a good role model; if you take a long time to make decisions or to pass work to your team members you are showing them that procrastination is acceptable practice.

Productivity

What everyone says they want to improve. Research shows that, other than having a good time management system, the key factors which influence productivity are:

1 Reward systems.
2 Variety of work.
3 Availability of advice.
4 Open information systems.
5 Individual autonomy.
6 Healthy work environment.
7 Adequate training and development.
8 Valid performance feedback.
9 Fluid organisation structure.

Profit and loss testing

A way of evaluating tasks. Ask these three questions for each task and then decide whether it is worth doing:

1 What is the 'profit' of this task if I do it?
2 What is the 'loss' if I don't do it?
3 What is the profit or loss if I do it differently?

Progressive dressing

A way for busy people to find the belongings they need each day. To progressively dress, have a path that you follow to get to your shower or bed. As you walk in the door kick off your shoes and drop your keys on the first table you come to. Now go into the next room and put your briefcase on the floor, put your coat over the arm of a chair, or hang it on a hook in the next room, and so on. In the morning you can retrace your steps to dress again quickly. For the frequent traveller this works particularly well in strange hotel rooms.

Progressive filing

A system for holding and maintaining papers for a lengthy activity. First devise your **categories** and dates. Then set up a folder for each 'progressive' stage and move your papers through the file as the project progresses.

Project management

A logical process which helps define, plan and implement a project; a true test of time management skills. Successful project management requires a balance of strategy and tactics because of the mix of technical, financial and human factors. Research by Dennis Slevin and Jeffrey Pinto reported in the *Sloan Management Review* Fall (1987) shows four kinds of problems that occur during project management: (1) action should have been taken and it wasn't; (2) action is taken and it shouldn't have been; (3) the wrong problem has been solved; (4) the right problem has been solved but the solution is not used.

A variety of project planning models are available. Here is an eight-step approach:

1 *Project mission defined*
   Goals and objectives are set, project is clearly defined and the reason for being and requirements for success are identified; evaluation mechanisms are projected and final deadline is set.
2 *Discussions and research*
   Senior management and client support gained to ensure

resources and authority are available; information is gathered to determine subsequent action.

3 *Planning*
Alternative approaches considered, overall plan is developed, progressions established, technological needs determined, project costs estimated and budgeted; monitoring, controlling and benchmarking systems formulated; trouble-shooting strategies devised; system for keeping management and clients regularly informed planned.

4 *Task breakdown*
Project is divided into manageable tasks, subtasks and blocks; work breakdown structure is devised and realistic estimates of action steps made which are required to complete the project; scheduling is completed and resources are allocated.

5 *Project team established*
Team is selected and trained; quality over quantity used for recruitment; sub-project managers established, performance expectations and monitoring explained; responsibility matrix completed which includes checkpoints and deadlines for individual tasks and project steps.

6 *Implementation*
Materials and resources are acquired, work is done and project monitored; modifications and trouble-shooting where necessary.

7 *Termination*
Unused resources are released, project is 'sold' to client; project team is reassigned.

8 *Evaluation*
Project is evaluated for timing and resource effectiveness, client satisfaction, and team and individual performance.

A variety of time-saving tools and aids can be used to help simplify management and tracking of a project. Use **Gantt charts** and network diagrams such as Program Evaluation and Review Technique (**PERT**) and Critical Path Method (CPM). Monitor less complex tasks using your **'to do' list** and **diary**. For recurring tasks, set up progressive card or **filing** systems. Wall **charts** allow you to visually track projects and come in a variety of sizes and styles. They can be magnetic with moveable components or ones which you can write on and/or **colour code** different sections of.

Set up a separate section in your **diary** or **planner** for each project. Keep a sheet of paper at the end of each project section for project-related phone numbers.

As an alternative or supplement to your project **planner**, a portable project workbook can help. This can easily accompany you to all briefings and consultations. Use a ring binder with dividers with sections for correspondence, staffing lists, tasks lists and schedules. Keep a copy on your desk.

Project management computer software can be a big time saver. Select carefully to find something that best suits your needs. Consider these factors:

1 Size and complexity of projects.
2 Hardware capabilities.
3 Sophistication versus ease of use.
4 'User friendly' manual in a reasonable size.
5 Quality and clarity of user documentation.
6 Ease of understanding project-status display screen.
7 Types of project plans available (Gantt charts etc.).
8 Ability to 'automatically' generate project plans.
9 Internal calendar and options to adjust it.
10 Options for project plan reports, cost reports, resource reports, variance reports.
11 Prerequisite project management knowledge.
12 Training needed.
13 Simple tutorial programs.
14 Reviews by people you know.

As the project progresses, time management intrusions can indicate trouble. Needing more memos with wider circulation can often be the first sign. Longer **'to do' lists** and late deadlines should also put you on the alert.

One of the biggest time wasters is a project that is interrupted or cancelled. This usually happens because of a change in direction by senior management. It is always a shock, not just for you but for the members of your project team. To prevent time being wasted in too much anger and frustration, tell your team up-front why it has happened and how it will affect new workloads. Finally, write up *in detail* exactly where you have left off in the project and where you would be going, stage by stage, if you were to continue. This will save you much time if management decides to revive the project at a later date.

Proxemics

The study of spatial configurations and interpersonal relations. Space needs to be functionally organised so that the arrangement of people and physical objects in the layout is appropriate. This physical arrangement can either support or hinder time management and the achievement of an individual's or the group's objectives. It also aids personal power and helps you to get your message across quickly.

For example, where is your desk located in relation to the doorway? If you face the doorway and people look into your office and you establish eye contact, you invite someone to interrupt you thus wasting time. On the other hand, turning your back to the door may be considered antisocial and, while it may save you interruption time in the short term, it may inhibit communication and cost you more time in the long term.

Where have you placed your visitors' chairs? When you're in someone else's office, try to move your chair to the side of the desk. Do you use chairs or have a couch? Chairs placed directly across the desk from you put you in a powerful position. You cannot easily be intimidated from that position. If your chair is a big one with arms and the visitors' chairs are smaller and without arms, this gives you even more authority. By contrast, if you come out from behind the desk and sit side by side with your visitor on a couch or use a group of chairs of equal size, then you will be seen as much more friendly and approachable.

Meetings held at a round table tend to be more participative than those held at a long table, although *where* people sit is likely to be more significant than the shape of the table. At a rectangular table, the head of the table is usually seen as the point of authority. Again, this may provide only a short-term solution to controlling time and, if the matter is not talked through, it may backfire thus costing you more time in crisis management.

Q

Quickie

Any self-contained task that can be accomplished in 5 minutes or less. Rather than doing a 'quickie', time is often wasted by rationalising that there are only a few minutes left before the meeting/lunch/end of day and that's not enough time to do anything. How many '5 minutes' do you waste during the day?

Why not spend 5 minutes making a list of tasks you can do in 5 minutes. Put it in a prominent place and use it frequently to keep up your **productivity**.

In 5 minutes or less you can write a thankyou note, make a telephone call, update your **'to do' list**, dictate a letter or memo, organise a file, read some **paperwork**, jot down a reminder in your **diary**. To help you form the 'quickie' habit, take 5 minutes now to make a list of 'quickie' tasks. Then every time you have a few minutes take out your list and do a 'quickie'.

Quiet time

A designated amount of time each day during which members of your team agree NOT to interrupt you. Tell colleagues that you are working on a system to give you time to be more productive. Even better, get the entire team to agree to simultaneously go onto quiet time.

The time allocated needs to be appropriate and can vary from half an hour for up to 2 hours. Lunchtime can be a good quiet time period. Most people are out and you can save time by eating out before or after the crowds. The rules of quiet time are:

1 No phone calls taken or made.

2   No visitors.
3   No paging.
4   No unnecessary talking or moving around.
5   No distractions and no **interruptions**.

Once you have accepted the concept of quiet time, agree on a codeword for emergencies and make sure only a few people have the code. Prepare a stop sign for your desk, door or adjacent wall which shows that quiet hour is on and says when you will be available again.

One of the pluses of quiet time is the 'rollover effect'. Once people get into the habit of making their own decisions and not interrupting you during quiet hour, chances are that they will continue this pattern for even longer than the designated time.

R

Rabbit chasers

People who run off in all directions to tackle any problem that beckons. To shed the rabbit habit, set **objectives** and plan. For an immediate solution, try using the strategy suggested for cigarette smokers trying to quit: wait 5 minutes before chasing a rabbit (lighting a cigarette). While you are waiting consider how much—or how little—value you will add to your time management health by chasing the rabbit.

Reading

That which either takes us too long or we never have enough time to do. Start your reading time management program by trying to substantially reduce what you have to read. A digest service can provide summaries of the latest in your field. Subscribing to a clipping service means that you will receive only those articles particularly relevant to your business needs. Then enrol in a rapid reading course to enable you to get through more material in less time.

Don't let reading build up, but rather take small 'bites' to keep the pile under control. To improve your reading habits learn to select, scan, spread, schedule and skim.

Select: To select what you should read, first survey and evaluate your reading in terms of your professional goals. As publications arrive ask yourself these six questions:

1 How long have I been receiving it?
2 How often do I do more than glance at it?
3 What will happen if I stop getting it?
4 How often does it contain something useful?
5 What provides the most value for the least reading time?

6 (If the organisation pays) would I pay for the subscription myself?

Then choose those two or three publications you want to read regularly and rotate the rest—perhaps every quarter.

If you paid for the subscription and own the publication tear out articles you want to read, place them in a folder and discard the magazine. If you only receive the publication on a circulation list and don't have time to read the article, cross your name off the list and write it in again at the bottom. When it comes back to you again, *if* you still want to read it take 15 minutes away from your desk to do it *that day*. Only photocopy in extreme circumstances. As you collect material for your 'to read' file, mark everything with a 'read by' date and shed items if they are unread by that date.

Scan: Once you have cut down the amount of reading that comes to your **desk**, you then need to scan to decide what you will read, what are the **priorities**, and what you will discard. To scan means to look for the general picture to decide whether you want to read in detail. Search for logic, ideas, major points. Check the table of contents, the index and any summaries, digests or abstracts. Scan the headings and sub-headings. Sixty-eight per cent of key ideas are usually in the first sentence of each paragraph with another 23 per cent of key ideas in the last sentence, so read the first and last sentence of any major paragraph. Carefully read the final paragraph or conclusion.

Spread: Try spreading the reading workload. As you scan, flag and circulate articles of interest to staff or ask staff to scan for you. Ask subscribers who already scan periodicals to mark them for you. Tell senders of reports to flag the important parts for you.

Schedule: To start your new routine, allocate a time and a place for your reading. Read in any place except at your desk, otherwise you may use reading as an excuse for **procrastination** and not tackling your A priority. Next, schedule a regular reading time in your **diary**. Make this a 'low' part of the day and set a time limit. Fifteen minutes on a regular basis is better than an hour 'sometime'.

A timer can help you concentrate, particularly if you limit attention to one article or item for 10 minutes. Some people have perfected the art of reading while they walk. Try it as a form of **doubling up** and combine brain exercise with body exercise. Keep a reading file in your **briefcase** and read while travelling, commuting, waiting for an appointment. Some people have made the choice to travel by public transport just so they can have reading time.

Skim: Once you have decided that you want to read something, use the skimming method to do it quickly. The average reading time of adults is between 200 and 300 words per minute. Your aim is to bring your speed up to at least 500 words per minute. Using the sweep, brush and hum techniques will help.

Sweeping is a preview technique which prevents the eye from stopping and starting. With the hand relaxed, sweep down the middle of each page letting your eyes drift gently to search for ideas. Your objective is to read thought patterns not words. Having swept over the article or chapter, go through it again *brushing* each line. Brushing means using three fingers and brushing along under each line with your hand 'underlining' what you are reading. As you progress, gradually speed up and eventually you will start to brush three or four lines at once. Most people silently pronounce words to themselves as they read. This slows down reading considerably. To prevent this, try *humming* to yourself while you read. The humming makes it more difficult to 'say' the words.

Technical reading requires special methods. Always read last things first—summaries and conclusions—then prefaces and introductions. Then glance through any charts, graphs or pictures. Do your first scan and then scan a second time using a soft pencil to make checkmarks in the margins about points to look up later or passages to read again. You can always erase these marks. Stick a Post-it note on the cover to jot down pages or sections you want to refer to later. For even greater retention, draw a **mind map** of the key ideas.

Red light time

A term used to indicate time when you do not want to be interrupted. (See also **Drop-in visitors**, **Interruptions**, **Quiet time**, **Green light time**.)

Re-entry

Physically and emotionally returning to work after a trip. How you approach your first day on return can make a big difference to your time management.

Consider your body clock, **prime time** and jet lag before you decide whether you want to attack or defend. An *attack* approach means getting up early and going straight into your exercise routine. Get to your desk at least 30 minutes earlier than you would normally, set your day's **objectives** and start working on your highest priority. This gives you a head start before team members drop in to say 'welcome back'. Leave your in-tray until later in the day. If you delegated well prior to your departure there should not be much in the tray anyway.

The opposite way of making your re-entry is *defensive*. Take the first morning to catch up on personal chores. Do some 'life administration', practise your relaxation or meditation and start back at work later in the morning or in the early afternoon.

Reference material

Books, papers, notes which you refer to on a regular basis. These need to be collected and put in a convenient location. Try using a **desk workbook**. Put reference books such as street and business directories, dictionaries etc. conveniently to hand, but with only those which you refer to on a daily basis on your desk—and even then out of your immediate work area.

Referral slip

Functional and practical form for referring or circulating information to specific staff members. Have the form made up in a bright colour and with a pleasant design to attract attention. Print the names of all your team members, but leave space to add any extra people to the list.

Leave a place for the date, and extra space at the bottom of the form for any special points you might like to make. To make it even faster to use, list some basic message boxes which you can tick, e.g. 'for information only', 'let's discuss', 'please do', etc. If you want the information to move quickly, add two columns after the name—one for the date received and one for the date passed on.

The last spot on the slip should indicate where the item is supposed to go next: rubbish, files, library. If you want the item back, add your own name last, and a 'return by' date. When the item is returned you can identify who sits on material for too long and perhaps make some changes in your routing methods.

Relaxation

A way of turning off, diverting and detaching yourself from work and **stress**. Harvard University cardiologist Herbert Benson calls this 'The Relaxation Response' and details his ideas in the book by the same name. Commonly used relaxation techniques include meditation, progressive relaxation, guided imagery and self-hypnosis.

Healthy time managers take time to relax as they know that a buildup of stress in the body will result in increased fatigue and loss of **productivity**. Regular relaxation breaks will also improve overall health and job satisfaction. There are four basic categories of relaxation 'activities':

1 Rests and diversions.
2 Active physical exercise.
3 Passive physical relaxation.
4 Deep relaxation.

Diversions include reading a book, seeing a film, chatting with a friend, having a short nap, taking a **joy break**. Walking, jogging, yoga, swimming, tennis, golf, bicycle riding and aerobics are all forms of active exercise. Of course, you may use these exercises for physical fitness as well as relaxation. Massage, physical manipulation, sexual activity and acupressure are all forms of passive physical relaxation. Deep relaxation or meditation consists of focusing your attention gently on some object or process without forcing things and surrendering thoughts for a brief time.

When a situation is stressful and intense, take a 10-minute

relaxation break instead of trying to press on regardless. Once you have relaxed you will probably be able to do what you need to do in much less time and with your mind clearly focused on the task. For quick relaxation techniques try these:

1　Alternate deep and shallow breathing for 5 minutes.
2　Tell a joke to a colleague.
3　Massage your forehead, eyes and back of your neck; if you can do so comfortably, take off your shoes and massage your feet.
4　Take a short walk.
5　Call a friend for a quick chat.
6　Go outside and scream.
7　Punch a soft pillow hard at least 10 times.
8　Close your eyes and imagine yourself sitting by a gently trickling stream with a beautiful mountain in the distance; stay that way for 5 minutes.
9　Take a 5-minute nap.

Reports

Documents frequently prepared for the psychological benefit of the writer rather than the business needs of the reader. **Reading** a report can sometimes be compared to stepping into quicksand; once you're in, there is more and more sand and it seems impossible to get out.

The first rule of report writing is not to write one in the first place. To do this, trust people to report exceptions. (See also **MBE** and **Delegation**.) Eliminate all written reports of a routine nature by encouraging autonomy and face-to-face reporting. If you have been caught in a GYR ('guard your rear') environment where everything gets written down for purposes of self-protection, start putting more **energy** into developing a climate of trust rather than writing more reports.

To time-manage your reports, look at them from five different perspectives: auditing; eliminating; reading; writing; simplifying.

1. Auditing
Before you can eliminate unnecessary reports, you need to conduct an audit to determine those that are useful and those that are not. To do a simple audit, post samples of all your

department's reports on a bulletin board. Then ask team members to initial any report they think needs to be continued and to write in one sentence or less why they believe it needs to be written.

For a more detailed audit, prepare a report questionnaire form and audit all reports received/written for a month. Keep it simple, with as many 'tick the box' questions as possible. Ask for information about the following points, and any others specific to your department's needs:

1 Frequency? Just in time? Too early? Too late?
2 Needed for **decision making**?
3 Time taken for preparation?
4 People involved in preparation?
5 Method of preparation? (form/computer/dictated)
6 Number of copies prepared? Names of recipients?
7 Would a circulation copy be sufficient?
8 Clear, easy to read?
9 Data accurate? Up to date? Too much? Not enough?
10 Value on a scale of 1 to 10?

As part of your audit, cost a sample of reports to determine a weighted average cost per page. Consider average hourly rates of pay for those involved, including writer(s) and keyboard people. Then add in cost of paper, printing and/or photocopying. To get an even better picture of the real cost of a report, incorporate rental costs per hour of floor space for people and equipment, heating, lighting. If you are feeling brave, include the average *reading* cost as well.

2. *Eliminating*
Once you have completed your auditing, decide which reports can be eliminated. For those reports which originate outside your immediate span of control, review each one and ask yourself whether reading the report will help you achieve your key **objectives** or whether it is needed for decision making. If the answer is '**no**', get yourself off the circulation list. If you think you might need parts of a report, ask an assistant to read it and highlight the important sections. Even better, delegate the reading of the report completely and trust team members to tell you about anything they think you need to know.

Consider whether your team members will get any value

from reading a report. If not, suggest that they take themselves off the circulation list.

If you are uncertain about whether you will need a report or not, or are in the early stages of your new report elimination procedures, file all your reports without reading them and keep a running list of the topics for quick reference. Better still, just keep a running list of the topics and the source. Then you will know where to look for the information if you need it and thus eliminate your need to file it.

Finally, offer financial rewards and other incentives for ideas about eliminating reports.

3. Reading

Practise all of your best rapid reading techniques when you receive reports. If you have asked your assistant to summarise or flag key items, read only those. Tear out those sections which will be useful and read or file only those. Refuse to read any report that does not have a summary page.

4. Writing

To speed your report **writing**, use **prime time** when your mind is most alert and your ideas come quickly. The fastest method of 'writing' your report is to dictate it instead. Remember that speaking is always faster than writing. Try to keep it to 3 minutes (that's roughly the equivalent of 750 written words or two to three double-spaced typed pages). When finished, circulate your *tape*. You can label, file and reuse tapes also.

For a variation of the above, quickly dictate a rough draft and work with the draft or, better still, get your assistant to finalise it from your rough.

Divide your report into manageable portions using the journalist's five Ws and an H: who, what, when, where, why and how. Or try this for a quick writing technique:

1 Write each heading or key idea on a large index card (12.5 × 20 cm) or on a separate piece of paper.
2 Put each diagram/chart/picture on a separate card/page.
3 Make rough outline points under each heading/key idea leaving space between each.
4 Fill in details under each point.
5 Shuffle the cards/pages until you have the right order, then write. (See also **Clustering**.)

5. *Simplifying*

Try to devise standard formats for your reports. Use **checklists**, fill-ins, standard paragraphs and computerisation. Invent methods to check that the data included are up to date as well as timely, accurate, appropriate and of the right quantity. Not enough information is just as useless as too much.

Try to keep all reports to a maximum of three pages. If someone (hopefully not on *your* team) wants to attach 110 pages of appendices to their report that's their prerogative. Insist that no report is circulated without a summary page.

Resource file

Index cards in a box or a Rolodex for 'at a glance' information. List contacts, support services, client information, anything you might need for quick reference. Use dividers to separate sections. This can double as a card file. Staple business cards and also write any extra information onto the index card.

Responsibility

The obligation to undertake a specific task or duty. To be effective, the person assigned the responsibility must agree to accept it. Responsibility without authority will often lead to dissatisfaction and poor productivity. (See also **Delegation.**)

Responsibility chart

A device used to keep track of tasks and responsibilities. It may consist of tasks and responsibilities which have been delegated or tasks assigned or agreed to by people in a group (see figure 14).

Reverse delegation

A way of turning an assigned task around so that the manager ends up completing it. Some team members become so expert at this that the manager ends up working for them rather than

Figure 14   Responsibility chart

RESPONSIBILITY CHART

Goals: 1. To place responsibility
        2. To include all involved persons

TASK: To develop a plan for enlarging the employees' lunchroom

Components of Task	Your Name	Jim Jones	Sarah Cane	Betty White	Al Franks	Alice Black									
	D														
Determine size and Capacity	S/W	CO			CO										
Kitchen facilities	S		W												
Location	S			W											
Lunchroom personnel	S	W													
Draw up plan	A	W													

Persons Involved

(After you have finished filling in the chart, re-think all persons who are involved in each category. If all involved persons have been assigned, place a check mark in the box for that category.)

Code:

✓ D - Director (has general responsibility, sets policy, establishes limits, etc.)

✓ S - Supervisor (supervises and assigns work, sees that job is done)

✓ W - Worker (does the work)

✓ CI- Consultant/Imperative (must be consulted)

✓ CO- Consultant/Optional (may be consulted)

✓ NI- Notify/Imperative (must be notified)

✓ A - Approver (must approve or disapprove completed task)

Source: Helen Reynolds & Mary E. Tramel, *Executive Time Management,* © 1975

130

Figure 15 Reverse delegation

Cause of reverse delegation	Suggested strategy
Open door policy; too easy to contact you.	Close the door; locate the worst offenders as far away from you as possible.
Team member doesn't like taking risks and lacks confidence.	Point out advantages of risk taking; reward risk; delegate in small steps; give frequent positive feedback; controls.
Task/problem is difficult to solve.	Check level of ability of team member; assign task to pair; ensure appropriate training available.
Team member is afraid of criticism and failure.	Assign carefully and clarify each step; have regular follow-up and controls; assign small sections; give regular positive feedback.
Failure to coordinate work.	Check own delegation skills; show team member how to draw up responsibility charts/coordination charts; keep charts visible.
Team member lacks information and resources.	Review your delegation techniques; responsibility without authority and without resources doesn't work.
Avoidance of higher level contacts.	Make introductions personally or via memo to support team member; explain value of contacts in terms of likely success of project, political and career value, power; bring 'hidden agendas' out into the open.
Boss wants to be needed and can't say 'no' to requests for help.	Practise saying 'no'; feed **monkeys** only at regular intervals.
Task assigned to wrong person.	Check own delegation techniques; provide training.

the other way around. If it's your team member doing the reversing, this will have a dramatic effect on your time management. Figure 15 shows some causes of reverse delegation and some strategies for coping with it.

131

Right angler

Someone so concerned with neatness and how things look that they delude themselves into believing that they are organised. Sunny Schlenger and Roberta Roesch in *How to be Organized in Spite of Yourself* say that 'Right Angling encourages (1) saving things you don't need, (2) losing valuable storage or display space, (3) allowing things to "sink roots" in the wrong places, and (4) having a nonfunctional and inefficient system'.

Right anglers have an overdeveloped need for control and equate this control with efficiency. They believe that straight edges, 'right angles' and neat and tidy desks are the most important part of time management. To them, straightening and cleaning means getting the job done.

If this description fits your personal style, look for storage products that look neat and *are* efficient. Log the time it takes you to locate something and evaluate whether it is worthwhile. Check to see that your systems are functional as well as 'beautiful'.

Roles

The part(s) you have chosen to fill in your social or business settings. We all fill many roles—businessperson, parent, child, friend, community worker. Most of us suffer from role conflict at some stage in our lives, some of us suffer continuously. Role conflict leads to time conflict. Choosing to stay later at work to finish a project, rather than going to have dinner with your parents, creates a role conflict.

Roger Merrill in *Connections* suggests that such conflict arises because we have not clarified our goals and what we want to achieve. 'Roles must, of course, be in harmony with and grow out of your personal **mission statement**', says Merrill. He advises writing a personal mission statement. Once your mission is stated and understood you can set clear **goals** or **objectives** in relation to it. Then identify the one, two or three most important things you can do in each role during the next year, based on the principles and values in your mission statement. As you work towards the goals in your roles you will experience less conflict *and* less guilt.

Routine

Responsibilities which we either avoid or on which we spend too much time. There can be psychological as well as physical benefits in established routines. The secret of mastering routine is to find some sort of system which enables you to maintain a balance between the routine and the tasks which lead to your key **goals** and **priorities**.

The left-brain dominant (see **Brain dominance**) person feels organised and gets a sense of well-being from a good routine. They have no problem establishing procedures and following them to the finest detail. The risk is that they overdo the detail and get caught up in routine for routine's sake, rather than focusing on more important targets.

The right-brain dominant person feels uneasy with routine and wants to be doing something else. Establishing a regular time each day in which to handle their routine work will be difficult. They need to build some routine into their schedule without overdoing it. Fifteen minutes a day may be enough.

Try doing your routine tasks in a setting which makes you feel good. Take out your colourful 'props'—those which you have specially purchased to make your routine more pleasant. While you are working, record any ideas that come to you on bright coloured cards or in a specially designated folder so you won't forget them. Use Post-it notes for reminders and have a visible place where you can stick them. Work with a partner to help you devise procedures. Then find a simple way to reward yourself when finished.

S

Sales time

The best return you can get for the sales you make in proportion to the time invested. The salesperson's time management starts with knowing who are the high payoff customers and prospects. Once you have identified them you can apply Pareto's **Eighty–twenty rule**.

To be an effective sales time manager you need to know the answer to these questions:

1   How many calls does it take to get each prospect?
2   How many prospects does it take to get each sale?
3   How many calls does it take to each existing account to keep it active?
4   What is the return or potential return on time invested for each customer and prospect?

To find out, start by keeping a **time log**. Do it for at least two weeks to get the full value. You may wish to make modifications in the standard log for those items specific to your job. Once you have analysed the results, you can then begin to calculate who are your 20 per cent of customers and 20 per cent of prospects who will bring you the highest return for the time invested.

Start your day by knowing where the calls will be before you leave home or the office in the morning. To use your sales time even more effectively:

1   Plan and prepare thoroughly.
2   Use waiting time to plan and catch up on **reading**.
3   Use **travel** time to make calls on your mobile **telephone**, listen to tapes on sales and **motivation** or dictate letters and memos.

4 Don't 'drop-in' on customers or prospects; confirm all **appointments**.

5 Treat a sales call like a meeting: never start it without identifying the finishing time—to yourself and to the customer.

6 Don't talk too much. It takes more time and puts the customer offside.

7 Take time to identify the decision makers. Selling to the wrong person wastes time giving your sales pitch to someone who can't settle things with you.

Sampling of work activity

A means of employing random observations whereby you can find out the ratio of the *amount of work* performed during a given period to the *amount of delay* that occurred during the same period. Thanks to the law of probability, if a sufficiently large sample of valid random observations of a work process are made, the data that are gathered are considered to be as reliable as if the work process were observed *continuously* over the period.

The technique consists of random, intermittent but frequent spot-checking of an activity and the recording of what is actually happening at the moment it is observed. From the sample of work obtained, the time spent on each type of operation in relation to the total time available is determined. If the sampling is done correctly, and a substantial number of observations (perhaps 100 or more) are made over a five-day week, the results will be statistically valid.

You can use time sampling for members of your own team and for yourself. Use preprinted **forms** or design your own. Once you have completed your sampling, analyse the findings and make any changes which seem advisable.

Scheduling

A way of specifying the sequences in which work is performed. Scheduling can be applied 'formally' to manual work or 'informally' to professional and clerical work. You can develop 'formal' schedules in a 'straight line', in parallel or by using critical paths. The most time-efficient way to schedule is to use one of the readily available scheduling tools such as **Gantt charts**, **PERT charts** or milestone charts.

For your 'informal', day-to-day schedules, try to follow these basic rules:

1 Plan your schedule at the same time every day; if you work with a secretary or assistant, do your scheduling together.
2 Put the schedule in **writing**, select a **calendar** or **diary** that you like, and keep it with you at all times.
3 Consider **prime time** and schedule most creative work and vital activities during peak periods.
4 Focus on **objectives** and do high priority tasks first.
5 Group like tasks.
6 Schedule in **blocks**.
7 Schedule **quiet time** if at all possible.
8 Use transition time productively.
9 Schedule thinking time every day.
10 Allow some flexibility for the unexpected.

Secretary's time

Time which is most frequently wasted by the manager. Good secretaries can act as team member, gatekeeper and time manager. Unfortunately most managers won't let them do this, thus wasting their own time as well as that of their secretary. General guidelines for time management apply to the secretary's time, including goal or objective setting, **planning**, paper, desks and **diary** management.

Start your new boss–secretary time management approach by agreeing to talk together about what you mean by '*team*'. Clarify expectations and explain office procedures and **objectives**. Establish new routines and ask for suggestions for time management. Set two one-week periods during the year when time **logs** will be kept. Mutually agree on systems and guidelines for the supervision of anyone reporting to the secretary.

Acknowledge responsibility and authority for delegated tasks and *don't overmanage*. Ask your secretary what other things might be delegated. Consider delegating all of your 'B' priority work to your secretary. (It is understood that your secretary is

136

already dealing with your 'C' priorities.) Allow provision for authority to use temporary help within agreed budgets.

Devise a system for keeping the channels of communication open. A *monthly performance/progress meeting* can help. Agree that you will both prepare a list of items/tasks for discussion and negotiate what needs to be changed, added or upgraded. Building a *daily planning meeting* into your routine is essential. Allocate five to ten minutes at the beginning of each day for this. During the meeting:

1   Discuss reallocation of **priorities**.
2   Check diaries.
3   Consider plans affecting department workload.
4   Clarify action/diary changes resulting from meetings.
5   Review messages from **telephone** calls and **'drop in' visitors**.
6   Highlight any potential office problems.
7   Agree on time needed to complete assigned tasks.

A secretary can save time in the way **meetings** are handled. Instead of only expecting preparation of **agendas**, rooms and materials, why not let your secretary attend some meetings and make notes in your absence?

Don't underutilise your support person's capacity to handle your in-tray. *Incoming* documents can be opened, scanned, read and sorted. In addition your secretary can:

1   Make calendar notations.
2   Annotate in margins.
3   Underline, highlight or flag key words and phrases.
4   Pull accompanying files.
5   Draft a response.
6   Summarise a long report.
7   Re-route to others.
8   Throw things away.

For *outgoing* documents your secretary can:

1   Do research.
2   Draft replies.
3   Proofread.
4   Edit.
5   Sign and send documents in your absence after you have approved the draft.

Use your secretary's time wisely when making travel arrangements. Even if you use a travel agent, put your secretary in control and let her or him make the intelligent decisions on your behalf. During your travel planning meeting provide this information:

1 Date of departure and return.
2 Travel time preferences.
3 Anyone accompanying you.
4 Desired class of service and seat preferences.
5 Choice of airports overseas (some cities have more than one).
6 Stopovers or nonstop.
7 Methods of payment (credit cards, etc.).
8 Accommodation required; hotel and room preferences.
9 Rental car requirements; size and options.
10 Method of transfer from arrival point to accommodation or other destination.
11 Amount of travel advance required.

Having a complete, detailed **itinerary** can save you considerable time. This should include dates, times, addresses, phone and fax numbers and general client information. Take at least two copies with you, one for your briefcase and one for your pocket or purse. Prior to departure, agree on the systems to be used for handling mail and telephone calls. Having an action log prepared, which shows who, what, when and what action was taken in your absence, can save considerable time upon your return.

Establish ground rules with your secretary for dealing with telephone calls and drop-in visitors. Agree on a system for answering and placing calls. Have a list of VIPs whose calls and visits you will always take. Your secretary should know which calls to re-route to others, which calls should have a message taken with arrangements made to return the call, and which calls should be put straight through to you. Secretaries complain that two of their biggest time wasters are not knowing the whereabouts of their boss and being interrupted by their boss when the boss doesn't have enough to do. Are you guilty?

Shared secretary
What if you share a secretary or support person. In today's environment this is highly likely. Expect conflict, and recognise

that it is just too hard for the secretary to be expected to resolve it. The team (this includes the secretary) needs to agree on ground rules. Rank, tasks or priorities may each require special consideration. Here are four systems that seem to work.

1 *First come, first served.* This system is simple and easy to manage. Each assignment is dated and goes to the bottom of the pile and is dealt with in turn.
2 *Time division.* The approach is to assign each team member a time slot for their work.
3 *Priority system.* Decide on a priority system in which everyone is clear about the meaning of the word 'URGENT'. Make certain that power games are not being played in relation to who gets what done when.
4 *Topical division.* Each work group has certain activities which are more important than others. The secretary puts the tasks in order according to a predetermined importance order.

Also agree on a system for collecting phone messages and noting who is 'in' and who is 'out'. Letting everyone do their own photocopying will also save the secretary's time.

Selective delay

A deliberate choice *not* to do something. This might be because your **stress** level is high and you need a break. Or perhaps you recognise that it's better to think about something for a while before you act. Deliberate delay is one of the few occasions when **procrastination** may be the best thing at the time. What makes the procrastination OK is the fact that you have made an active choice.

Shouldas

A 'Shoulda' is almost a Siamese twin to the **Gonna**. 'Shouldas' waste an inordinate amount of time and **energy** feeling guilty and worrying about what they 'shoulda' done. You need them like you need the bubonic plague. 'Shouldas' are always sorry afterwards because they 'shoulda' done something and didn't.

They are emotionally immobilised by guilt and worry. This guilt is a cop-out and an excuse for not being effective. 'Shouldas' can always find an excuse for their inactivity.

If *you* are a 'Shoulda', make a list now of ten things you are avoiding doing and start doing them one by one. Replace guilt and worry with action planning. Spend some time setting down some meaningful **goals**.

If you have a 'Shoulda' working as part of your team, don't accept excuses or show any pity for lack of results. You will just reinforce their excuses for not changing. Instead, state clearly and firmly what it is you expect when you set a task. Ensure that guidelines, deadlines, controls and punishments for non-performance are understood. You may need to ask a 'Shoulda' to repeat parrot fashion what they have understood by an assignment. Follow up in **writing** if necessary. If they pull a 'shoulda' on you again, act by giving immediate feedback. Record the assigned task and the results and let the 'Shoulda' know that it is in writing. Then take other action you feel is appropriate.

Siberia sendoff

The next step toward getting rid of unwanted 'drop-ins' without actually shutting the door in their face. To avoid getting a reputation for being 'difficult', practise 'closed door' hours or remove yourself to 'Siberia', a quiet spot where you can work undisturbed. Use the library or a conference room—or even rent a nearby hotel room if you are desperate. (See also **Interruptions**.)

Simplified letter

A style of letter which can save more than 10 per cent in keying time alone. The American Administrative Management Society has been promulgating this for years and it is finally beginning to catch on. In this form, every line starts at the left margin (see figure 16). This minimises use of space bar and tabulator key. There is no salutation. There is also no 'Yours faithfully', with only the name and title of the originator of the letter being keyed.

140

Figure 16   Simplified letter

---

23 June 1993

Mr Nikolas Skoufis
21 Windsor Avenue
Oakleigh South VIC 3167

SIMPLIFIED LETTER STYLE

You have written to ask about the simplified letter style which is the most modern style and incorporates several interesting features.

This letter is produced in full block style with every line starting at the left-hand margin. The letter always starts with a subject line which is keyed in all capital letters. There is no salutation or complimentary close. The author's names and official title are in capital letters also.

The advantage of this letter is the ease of keyboarding, creating maximum efficiency of time.

LYNNE WENIG
MANAGING DIRECTOR

LW/PW/183

There is another way you can simplify your correspondence and become more global at the same time. Many Europeans show the date by putting the year, the month and the day (1993-8-12) on their letters rather than writing 12 August 1993. Not only is this faster but it provides a basic guide for filing and storing the communication.

Speed writing

A system of rapid writing where you lv out unesry vwls & cnsnts. U abrev whn poss & dvlp shrt cts.

Sprinting concept

A tricky means of pushing yourself to be more productive. One sprinting method is to use your time **log** *in reverse.* Fill out your log a day ahead and plan it to the minute. As you go through the day, check every half-hour or so to see if you are on time. If not, speed up or move to the next item on your schedule. Try this for two or three days.

A second sprinting method is to pick a few days in a row to work with all the speed you can summon. Make them long days, starting early and working late. Don't stop to review your day or re-do anything—just sprint. After three or four days, return to your normal schedule. If the sprinting concept worked you will be faster and more efficient.

Stacked desk syndrome

A style often preferred by right-brain dominant people (see **Brain dominance**) whereby everything is kept out on the **desk** so that you 'don't forget anything'. Right-brain dominants also like the visual stimulation. Other people who show symptoms of the stacked desk syndrome have deep-seated psychological needs. Stacks of paper can make you feel important—'see how busy I am with all this paper to get through'. They can also provide a good hiding place—'no one will ask me to do anything if they can't see me'. If you have an assistant get that person to keep your desk clear. If not, get help from an 'expert' colleague to create a simple **filing**/storage system. Try using **G.U.T.S.**

Stalling

Delaying and calling 'time out' until you decide whether you can't, won't or are not interested in doing something. This is a useful technique for the less assertive person who has difficulty saying '**no**'. Ask for 24 to 48 hours to 'think it over'. Don't be pressured into giving an immediate response. While stalling, ask yourself:

1 Why have they asked *me*?
2 Do I have the time and the **energy** to do it?
3 Is the job/task/activity necessary?
4 Does it fit in with my **objectives**?
5 What's in it for me?

Standard data

See **Time measurement**.

Star diagram

A picture which summarises a theme and its main points. This is a useful technique to make quick notes about something you are reading or to which you are listening. You can then use the star diagram for review (see figure 17). The method could be described as a more controlled form of **mind mapping**. The diagram consists of a centre, which contains the

Figure 17   Star diagram

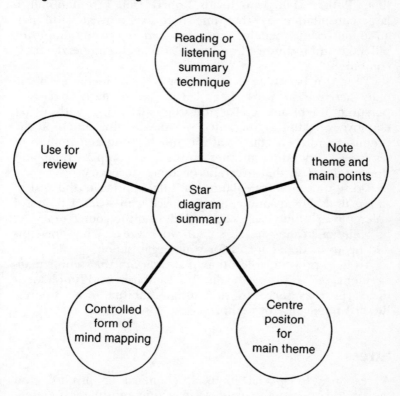

main theme in your own words, and the 'points' of the star with the key ideas.

Start time

A simple formula for encouraging good time management. When doing your scheduling, write in the *start* time as well as the finishing time. It is also an effective anti-**procrastination** aid.

Stolen time

The deliberate and persistent abuse and waste of paid work time. Robert Half, who heads Robert Half International, a large consultancy, says that time theft takes a greater toll than all other crimes against business (ranging from employee pilferage and insurance fraud to kickbacks and embezzlement) combined.

Time can be stolen in a number of ways, including habitually arriving at work late, leaving work early, excessive personal **telephone** calls, non-stop socialising with other employees, taking unwarranted sick days, eating lunch on the premises and then going out for 'lunch', long and numerous tea breaks, operating another business on company time, and slowing down so that overtime becomes necessary.

Do some simple calculations to fully appreciate the cost of stolen time. For example, an employee who steals 4 hours of an employer's time each week will, during the course of a year, be guilty of stealing nearly six full work weeks. What does this add up to in dollar terms for your organisation?

To help prevent stolen time make certain that senior management set a proper example. Establish and implement measures that serve to discourage habitual time thieves. Reward time-conscious employees.

Stress

A response to special physical, chemical or psychological demands placed upon you by an action or situation. These demands cause you to adjust, adapt or change. There are varying degrees and different forms of stress. What causes stress for one person may not even bother another.

Not all stress is bad for you. Stress comes in both *positive* and *negative* forms but unfortunately the body doesn't discriminate between the two.

There are obvious links between time management and stress. There is no way that someone can be expected to continue to work at maximum productivity while experiencing negative stress. A simple way to look at the complex subject of stress is to view it in terms of sources (stressors), symptoms and strategies.

Sources (Stressors)

Studies have identified the following as some of the main sources of negative stress found in organisations:

1 *Individually oriented stressors.* Examples include inability to manage time efficiently, lack of organisation, under- or over-estimating abilities, signs of failing in an assignment, physical and emotional impact of long hours, travel or deadlines, inability to delegate, inability to say '**no**', commuting time.

2 *Interpersonally oriented stressors.* Examples include inadequate support and demand for perfection from managers and supervisors, feeling that the boss is incompetent, inadequate performance from team members, dealing with aggressive or manipulative people, lack of autonomy, not being involved in **decision making**.

3 *Organisationally oriented stressors.* These can be grouped into four main categories as in figure 18.

4 *Technostressors.* Inability to adapt to computers or other hi-tech equipment. This can be characterised by underadaptation—when people feel overwhelmed and frightened by equipment—or overidentification—e.g. when people working with computers become so involved they simply don't stop working when they are tired. As well, there is the physical impact of the continued use of terminals.

Symptoms

Symptoms of stress are many and varied. Generally they group into five categories. Some of the symptoms can be:

Figure 18   Stress

Environment	Employee/ employer relationship	Job design	Socio- economic factors
overcrowding	lack of respect	rapid work pace	low pay
poor ventil- ation; smoke filled rooms	non-supportive boss	lack of control over time and work	dead-end job
excessive noise	too many bosses	constant sitting	job dissatisfaction
poor lighting; excessive glare	ineffective boss	repetitive tasks	sex, race, age discrimination
poor furniture design	high responsibility, little authority	inadequate rest breaks	job insecurity
	lack of recognition	heavy workload; long hours	inadequate childcare
	ineffective grievance procedures	underused skills	dual responsibility for home and work
	highly competitive atmosphere	unclear job requirements	inadequate career counselling
	poor professional communication systems	sudden changes from frantic activity to slow, boring pace	
	extremes of management style		
	inadequate credit for accomplishments		
	inadequate staffing levels		
	lack of feedback both positive and negative		

1 *Physical:* appetite change, headaches, tension, fatigue, insomnia, weight change, muscle aches, pounding heart, rashes, increased drug, alcohol or tobacco use.
2 *Emotional:* anxiety, frustration, the 'blues', mood swings, bad temper, irritability, depression, nervous laughter.
3 *Spiritual:* loss of meaning, doubt, being unforgiving, martyrdom, loss of direction, cynicism.
4 *Mental:* forgetfulness, low productivity, negative attitude, confusion, lethargy, boredom, negative self-talk, poor concentration.
5 *Relational:* isolation, intolerance, resentment, loneliness, lashing out, lowered sex drive, nagging, distrust, fewer contacts with friends.

Strategies

Having control or perceiving yourself as having control over negative outcomes reduces stress. Therefore stress needs to be *managed*, not simply avoided. Stress management is a decision-making process.

When you are feeling stress you can alter it, avoid it or accept it by building resistance or changing your perceptions of it. The ways in which we alter, avoid or accept stress are our *coping skills or strategies.* A negative coping pattern can make stress worse, and can lead to serious illness. Negative 'coping' strategies frequently include CATS: caffeine (including chocolate as well as tea and coffee), alcohol, tobacco or sugar. There is also a tendency to increase drug taking. Negative copers may also act as though nothing has happened, or even apologise for something when they are right.

There is a wide variety of positive coping skills and strategies and you need to identify those which will work for you. Here are 25 proven stress reducers you can try:

1 Get up 15 minutes earlier in the morning to avoid morning mishaps and arrive at work free of stress.
2 Try a massage or a hot bath.
3 Practise meditation and relaxation techniques; take plenty of short **joy breaks**; listen to music, cuddle a fluffy toy, look at a restful picture, sit and do nothing.
4 Don't rely on your memory. Write down **appointments** and reminders.

5 Be prepared to wait. Make use of waiting time by **reading** or listening to a tape on relaxation.

6 Organise your workspace so that you always know where things are.

7 Have a hobby that keeps you mentally and physically busy.

8 Find solutions to problems by **brainstorming**; decide on **priorities** and **goals**.

9 Eat proper meals, eat foods that please you, and restrict your intake of alcohol, caffeine and other drugs.

10 Keep a 'victory log'. Record anything from having a good meeting with the boss to losing half a kilo in weight. During the day review your victory log as often as your **'to do' list**.

11 Get or remain in good physical condition.

12 Creatively **visualise** positive outcomes and saying **'no'**.

13 Breathe deeply. Respond immediately to stress signals with deep breathing which reduces the effects of stress and helps get you in psychological control.

14 Schedule 30 minutes or more a day just to relax and be alone to think, read, write, reminisce, plan or dream.

15 Try some anti-stress minerals and vitamins, especially B-complex and the Cs.

16 Ask people for help or advice; unburden yourself to a friend or colleague.

17 Change your scenery. Take a walk or a jog around the floor or the block to get your circulation going.

18 Talk to someone about a topic not related to the source of stress; do something for others.

19 If a particularly 'unpleasant' task faces you, do it early in the day and get it over with. **Procrastination** is stressful.

20 Learn to **delegate** responsibility and authority.

21 Eliminate destructive self-talk: 'I'm too old to. . .', I'm not smart enough to. . .'

22 Plan ahead.

23 Do one thing at a time. When you are working on a project, concentrate on doing that project and forget about everything else you have to do.

24 Go to a stress management program.

25 When all else fails, laugh or cry. These are the oldest and most pleasant forms of stress relief known. Tears triggered by emotions contain a high concentration of proteins and they may actually carry away from the body the harmful

chemical by-products of stress. Laughter, too, seems to release endorphins and other chemicals which not only make us feel terrific but may reverse some of the damage of stress.

Subordinate tyranny

A severe form of **reverse delegation**. You are being subjected to subordinate tyranny when one of your team members says any of these:

* 'We've got a problem.'
* 'When can I have your approval?'
* 'Let's get together and talk about this.'
* 'Only you can handle it.'
* 'Can you send me a memo on that?'
* 'Can you draw up an initial draft I can look at?'

Success

Accomplishment, achievement, attainment or whatever you believe it to be.

Superwoman

A woman who is supposedly able to 'have it all' and 'do it all' with superb standards. This is a myth.

Swiss cheese method

A 'bits and pieces' approach. When you have a task that is overwhelming you, break it down into small, manageable steps. When you have completed one step, do the next. Gradually continue until you have completed the 'overwhelming' task. The holes in a Swiss cheese symbolise the bits and pieces. Some people prefer to 'slice the salami' or 'take small bites' ('work smarter not harder').

Synergy

A term used to describe the phenomenon that occurs when two or more actions combine in such a way that the whole is greater than the sum of its individual parts: e.g. $2 + 2 = 5$. When you are synergistic you are more effective.

T

Talent–time assessment

A useful method for conducting an inventory of staff skills and talents to match them with your department's or team's changing time and goal-achievement requirements. Merrill and Donna Douglass in *Manage Your Time, Manage Your Work, Manage Yourself* say that this is a 'useful tool for managers who feel the need for some reorganization in work assignments for their work group'. It can be used to help in **delegating** effectively, identifying training and re-training needs, and more readily meeting your own needs and those of your team. The Douglass's suggest this method:

1 Ask your staff to consider and list their special skills, likes and dislikes about work tasks, attitudes, and the good and bad features of their current job.
2 Objectively assess and modify the lists and enter staff members' talents and attitudes on 3 x 5 inch cards; put the members' names on the reverse side of their cards to avoid bias on your part during step 4.
3 On a set of cards of a different colour identify all activities required for the team to achieve its work **goals**.
4 Compare and match the differently coloured cards, and on this basis consider how you might reorganise your team's duties.

Tao of time

A concept of time management based on the Taoist belief that events and opportunities occur when and as they should. Diana Hunt and Pam Hait in the book of the same name say that the tao of time begins with the premise that time is limitless

151

and highly personal. They believe that you need to 'go within yourself' to establish your comfortable range of rhythms and balance.

The Tao philosophy is NOW-oriented. It suggests that living in the present time eliminates clock-induced stress. Instead of concentrating on schedules, you should learn to release yourself from the pressures of the clock and put all your **energy** into the job at hand.

Targeting

Ability to direct behaviour to recognised, predetermined **objectives**; the means through which you establish and pursue **goals**. Leon Tec in *Targets* says that the reason people have trouble achieving objectives is their 'inability to target'. A target is a good visual image to have to help you to plan.

To carry through your targeting, you need to sequence. Break down your compound targets into a series of interim targets. Then arrange the targets into an optimum sequence. A simpler way of putting it would be to say that B should follow A, C follow B and so on. This may seem obvious to you but how often do you try to do C before A?

Tear system

A method to make you more aware of how often you defy the 'handle each paper once only' rule. Each time you look at a piece of paper, tear a small piece off a corner. This tear will act as a powerful reminder to process the work once only. (See also **measles method**.)

Telecommuting

The substitution of telecommunications and computers for commuting to work. This development saves a lot of travel time for commuters. Two types of telecommuters are evolving. The first type are those who do away with the workday 'commute' entirely and turn a part of their home into an office. The second type are those who lessen the number of commutes by going to nearby regional offices that are tied by telecommunication systems to head office.

Teleconferencing

A meeting held by telephone which links a number of locations (locally, nationally or overseas) simultaneously. For the time-conscious businessperson it provides a convenient, quick exchange of information without the **travel time**. There are many worthwhile features of teleconferencing. In particular:

1 Sub-conferences can be held where small groups exit the main conference, talk privately and then rejoin the main conference. Ten separate conferences can be conducted simultaneously.
2 One or more participants can be connected to listen-only mode so they can hear but not speak. If requested the operator can change the connection to allow them to speak.
3 The whole conference can be recorded on tape, thus providing a transcript of the meeting.

Meetings are often non-productive because little thought has gone into the preparation—particularly who will participate and how the **agenda** will be formulated. With teleconferencing, where you are paying by the minute, proper preparation is crucial. Participants need to be ready for the call and must have received an agenda, visuals and handouts prior to the meeting.

If your meetings require the display of written proposals, graphs or financial figures, or if you want to watch 'body language' reactions, **Videoconferencing** may be a better alternative.

Telephone

A device which your internal and external customers, clients and colleagues use to contact you. They are usually seeking information or advice. Sometimes they are procrastinating and decide to ring you instead of working on their A priority. This 'interruption' wastes your time as well as theirs.

Start your telephone time management by selecting a machine with integrated functions, facilities and features. The larger the system the more options available, but even the most basic business telephone has some time management aids. Look for these:

1 *Memory dialling* which allows single or double touch dialling of your most frequently called numbers.
2 *Last number redial* which automatically stores the last number dialled, allowing redialling by one touch of the appropriate key.
3 *Alpha numeric key pad* which allows companies or individuals to be dialled using letters, e.g. ANSETT.
4 *Handsfree operation* which leaves you free to attend to other matters whilst the call is being connected; a built-in speaker lets you conduct a two-way conversation in the handsfree mode.
5 *Day, date, time* visually displayed.
6 *Timer* located in the display as well as an alarm function to remind you of that important date.
7 *Hold indication* that flashes on the display to indicate to the user that a call has been placed on hold.
8 *Automatic retry* which will automatically make up to ten attempts to call a busy number at 1-minute intervals.
9 *Combined telephone, answering machine and fax* which allows you access to the features of three items of equipment yet with only one device.
10 *Easycall compatible* which allows you to have two lines (and keep one caller on hold) on even the smallest telephone.

Mobile (cellular) phones
An indispensable time management tool of the trade for people whose job requires mobility. Many of the features of ordinary phones can be found on mobile phones as well. Popular time-saving features of mobile phones include:

1 *Visual display* which shows names and memory locations, messages, queries and warnings.
2 *Time talk meter* which tells the time elapsed in the current call, time taken by the last call and total time-on-air since

the timer was last reset. Some can be programmed to beep at regular intervals to help you keep track of time.

3 *Call in absence indicator* which tells you if an incoming call was received, the number of calls missed, and the time at which the last missed call occurred.

4 *Alphanumeric memory* in which you can store phone numbers and names, and which has an alphabetic directory that lets you scroll to the right name automatically.

5 *Portable handsfree* which allows you to put the phone on your belt or bag, connect a small cord to the phone and put the earplug in your ear to listen.

6 *Travel battery charger* which can be used from a 12V car cigarette lighter.

Mobile phone users have many time advantages. They are totally contactable and the phone acts as an extension to home and office phone facilities. This can save time, fuel and money. There is complete flexibility of making and receiving calls.

Call diversion allows you to re-direct calls to another number if wanted because you will be 'off line' or because you are seeking a few minutes of quiet solitude (something that becomes very elusive to mobile phone users). One of the biggest time savers is the capacity to ring before an appointment if you are going to be late and advise the person you are meeting. The handsfree feature allows you to talk while driving and if you should get lost en route you can call for directions from your mobile.

Logs

Start monitoring your **interruptions** by taking a **time log** of all telephone calls for one week. Then analyse them looking for patterns. For example, are the same people causing most of the interruptions? Are you receiving similar queries over and over again? Once you have this information you can design some prevention strategies.

Systems

Telephone time management starts with defining your system for both incoming and outgoing calls.

Incoming:

1 Have calls screened if possible; train the person who

answers the calls to ask the right questions so that they can re-route calls if possible.

2 If you have a secretary, delegate authority to handle routine calls. If you are not available, messages from important calls should be attached to relevant documents before being given to you.

3 Appoint certain staff as `liaison officers' for particular callers or clients.

4 Have an exchange or rostering system, where colleagues agree to take each other's calls during a designated period. This will leave you **blocks** of uninterrupted time.

5 Have a good system for keeping track of call-backs; use a message centre to keep messages in one place.

6 Give your assistant three separate lists of people and revise the lists regularly:

a   don't put through

b   talk to except during conferences or scheduled quiet hours

c   talk to any time

7 Have your assistant log calls on a special form, in a spiral-bound message book or on your computer. You can review the summary of calls quickly and decide which ones need a response from you and which can be delegated. This summary also provides a permanent record of incoming calls which can be used when evaluating their extent and causes. Then you can work with your team to devise ways of cutting down telephone calls.

8 Schedule specific times for incoming calls. Have whoever screens your calls ask callers to ring back only at specific times when you will be available.

9 Use an **answering machine** but think carefully about what you want your message to say—about you and about your organisation.

Outgoing:

1 Dial your own calls. This saves the time of three people: you, your assistant and the person you are calling who will otherwise waste time waiting for you to be connected.

2 Batch calls.

3 Plan outgoing calls carefully. Be prepared to present yourself and your background if necessary.

4 Make notes of the best time of the day/week to get through to people you phone on a regular basis; include this information in your directory.

5 When you have trouble reaching someone, telephone before or after hours. Many busy people come in early and stay late.

6 Make A-priority calls in the morning; less important ones at the end of the day.

7 Use telephone credit cards when you are travelling. This is faster and also provides you with a record of your calls.

8 Return calls just before lunch or just before people are ready to leave for the day. Conversations are faster then.

Messages
Think carefully about the messages you leave when the person you are ringing is unavailable. Each message should contain your name, your number, where you can be reached, the reason for your call and the best call-back time. 'Tell her I called' doesn't help very much. 'Tell her I've lined up the contact she asked for' is more likely to get a quick call-back. Put the message you leave on your **answering machine** to good use. When making a call-back appointment time, make it for a 15-minute period; for example, if a manager will be available at 11 am make an appointment to ring between 11 and 11.15.

Beginnings
You call them: Ask whether the person has time to spare—NOT 'Are you busy?' but 'Is this a good time to talk?'.

They call you: Set up the *end* of the conversation at the beginning by warning that time is limited. Ask the time required for the call and then negotiate. Try saying: 'I really can't spend a lot of time on the telephone today/now/this morning' or 'Let's speak briefly and then arrange to meet for lunch'. Then try these openers:

• What can I do for you?
• How can I help you?
• What do you need?

If you can't talk, say so. 'I'm not able to talk right now, so can I get back to you?' says it all. For the persistent, try:

• I have someone in my office.
• I'm just on my way out the door.

- I'm expecting a long distance call at any minute.
- Someone is waiting here to see me.
- 'I'll call you back', and then ring at the end of their day.

Endings

Try any of these:

- Before we hang up. . .
- My boss is waiting for me.
- I've got to be at a meeting in two minutes.
- Let me say, just before we hang up. . .
- I have another call and really must go.
- It's been good talking to you, but I have to get back to work.
- Is there anything else we need to talk about before we hang up?
- If that winds things up, I must get moving.

Some general hints

1 If the caller is long-winded, try letting them talk themselves out; silence tends to end a conversation sooner.
2 Make notes on your calls as they are just as important as face-to-face meetings.
3 Keep a clock or timer by your phone.
4 Stand up when talking to shorten call time.
5 Double up by doing some simple exercises or reading/opening mail while you are handling the call; a shoulder apparatus leaves your hands free.
6 Always give a specific call-back time so that you can consolidate your return calls.
7 Save up calls for your **telephone hour**.
8 Avoid playing **telephone tag**.
9 Limit the amount of time you are prepared to spend 'on hold'. After a reasonable amount of time, hang up.

Telephone hour

A specified hour of the day or week in which you focus on returning messages, making important calls, seeking information and keeping in touch with your network. This burst of concentrated work will enable you to complete far more than you would scattering your calls. When you have finished you will be free of most of your calls until the next telephone hour.

To get ready for your hour, save up your messages. Make certain you have necessary files, notes, writing implements to hand. A timing device might be useful. Choose the right time of the day for your calls. Most people are available during the first two hours of the morning and the last two hours of the afternoon, although you may need to modify this for people who work on flexitime. Experience has indicated that the best times to get executives are:

- 8.15–9.00 am
- 12.30–2.30 pm
- 5.00–6.00 pm

Test your times and be prepared to reschedule your hour if you are getting too many 'not available' responses. Keep notes on your calls. This is particularly important if you promise someone you'll call them back at a specific time.

Telephone tag

A giant time waster in which people keep leaving messages for each other because they are unavailable. To minimise telephone tag, follow these basics:

1 Improve your timing; schedule calls when you are most likely to reach people.
2 Develop second or even third contacts within organisations who can answer your questions instead of your original contact; if your contact has a secretary get to know them.
3 Don't be frightened to push to find out when your call will be returned or when it would be best to try again.
4 Think carefully about the messages you leave. Be creative. Clearly define what you need and your timeframe. Light humour can help.
5 Establish regular 'in office' hours so that people know they can contact you during that time.
6 Know when to quit. After a certain number of non-responses, try writing a letter.

Tickler file

The name given to a file used for **follow-up** and ready reference. The name comes from the way you 'tickle' the tabs looking for the right file. Tickler files may consist of folders or file cards and provide a daily reminder for matters that must be completed at some future date. The folders or cards are rotated daily so that the one for the current day is in front or on top.

With a folder system, copies of letters, memos or reports (or notes about those documents) that require follow up are filed in the tickler file under the follow-up date. Special reminder notes about tasks to be done on certain days can also be inserted in the tickler folder. If using a card system, the follow-up notations are entered on the appropriate card.

As part of your daily routine, check the tickler file for items that are to be handled that day. It also pays to check the next day's file to see whether there is a task that might be started early. (See also **Follow-up system**.)

Time budget

An itemised plan for how you will spend your time resource. Fran Tarkenton and Joseph Boyett writing in *Entrepreneur* advise making an 'inventory of the demands on your time and itemizing your expected time expenditures'. They recommend taking some ruled paper and dividing it into six columns. 'Label the columns: 1) daily, 2) weekly, 3) biweekly, 4) monthly, 5) quarterly, and 6) yearly. Under each column, list recurring activities you must perform according to their frequency, together with an estimate of how much time you need to allot for each activity'.

When you have completed the list, start budgeting your time. Start by making allocations for personal time such as time with family and friends and for regular exercise. Block out these times in your **diary**. What remains is your 'total available business time budget'.

Then start transferring your recurring business activities to your diary. Tarkenton and Boyett advise that you 'first enter those that have specific deadlines, then enter those that can be performed at any time during the day, week, month'.

Reserve some **blocks** of time each day for non-recurring tasks. Your diary now contains your time budget. This is your long-term plan. You can then go on to prepare your daily **'to do' list** which is your short-term plan.

Time horizon

An individual's time horizon is the picture of the future that the person not only vaguely thinks and talks about, but can actually deal with, forecast and control by doing things on a scale with which they feel comfortable. Most people find a comfortable time horizon without projecting much into the future. Time horizons will be shorter when conditions are unpredictable or an organisation is slow to adapt. When conditions are stable, or when the organisation can adapt easily, a long horizon is desirable.

Time horizon measurement

The working capacity of individuals can be viewed in terms of their ability to manage complexity of information and unexpected events over various spans of time in relation to a defined goal. Elliott Jaques describes this in his book *Requisite Organization*. Put another way, it is the farthest forward an individual can plan *and* achieve a stated goal. It is an indicator of that person's ability to handle both unexpected obstacles and information of varying degrees of complexity and usefulness.

Time horizon turns out to be an objectively measurable characteristic of each individual, and gives a direct measure of their current capacity to resolve a particular level of problem/goal complexity. There is evidence that the time horizon of individuals matures and develops in a systematic manner throughout life—from seconds in infancy to days, weeks, months and years in adulthood.

Time log

A device used to pinpoint the way in which time is being used.

Once a log has been completed the results can be analysed and any necessary corrective action taken. Despite the fact that the results of a log can provide the basis for a new time management program, the exercise tends to be avoided. This is because you 'just don't have the time'.

Time logs need not be complicated. Some experts suggest clarifying and classifying major weekly activities first, listing and numbering these, and then writing in the numbers as the week progresses. This may be a waste of time. If you make an appropriate record in your log, these activities will show up anyhow.

Start your log by drawing up a chart for yourself. In its simplest form the log needs only three columns: one for the time, one for the activity, and a big one for analysis notes (see figure 19). Leave space somewhere on the page for you to write your key goal(s) for the day. Be sure that you record **interruptions**, **appointments**, **meetings**, projects and **paperwork**.

You can preprint time intervals on the log if you wish, to make it even easier to complete. Every 15 minutes is probably reasonable although some prefer shorter or longer periods. With intervals longer than 15 minutes there is a high risk of the short time wasters being overlooked.

One useful variation of your log is to have columns for

Figure 19   Time log

| Date: MY TIME LOG |
| My key goal(s) for the day: .... |
| .... |

Time (add actual and estimated if desired)	Activity	Analysis

start time, estimated time, and actual time. This enables you to see how good you are at estimating how long an activity will actually take and then trying to account for the discrepancy. You can add columns for percentage effectiveness/whether the activity was planned/interruptions/priority. Or you can make up your own set of columns—whatever will work for you.

Reproduce enough copies of your log so that you have one for each day you are studying. Three is the minimum for a good study, and seven to ten ideal with one non-working day included. The log needs to be easily portable so think about size when you are designing it.

Start your log each day by listing your key **goal(s)** for that day. Then begin your recording when you get up in the morning and finish at the normal day's end. This enables you to record personal, family and professional activities. You can cheat of course. But trying to make yourself look good on your time log serves no purpose other than self-deception.

When you have completed logs for a reasonable number of days you can begin your analysis:

1 Look first to see whether your performance matched your goals. What percentage of time was spent on your key goals?
2 If you were recording estimated time, how accurately were you able to judge how long something would take to complete? How might you account for the discrepancies?
3 Make a list of all the activities over the period and total up the time per day (per week) for each. You may wish to work out the percentage of time spent on each activity.
4 How well did your daily activities match those of your job description?
5 How much time was spent in **planning**?
6 Was the amount of time spent on an activity worthwhile for the **productivity** gained?
7 Look at patterns. Were you doing the right thing at the right time, the right thing at the wrong time, or just the wrong thing?
8 How frequently were you interrupted? By whom? For how long?
9 How much time was spent on paperwork?
10 How much time was spent at meetings? How much of the meeting time was productive?

11 What could be delegated to someone else?
12 How much time was spent doing high payoff activities? **Low payoff activities**?
13 How much time was spent on **crisis management**? Could any of it have been avoided? How?
14 What systems were you using? How effective were they? Can you combine, simplify?

Once you have analysed your logs, begin planning ways you could reorganise your day. Don't try to change everything at once. Focus on one or two areas where you can see a high payoff.

Fix a period of time to test your strategies (one month/three months?) and then log yourself again. Add one or two more strategies. You may need to repeat this pattern three or four times until you start to get it right.

When you have reorganised *your* time, why not try a *work-group time analysis*? Start by constructing a log which lists predefined task **categories**. Ask group members to check the categories at various points during the day. Make it very clear to the group that this is going to be used to help identify what the group is really doing, and whether the right amount of time is going into the right tasks. It will NOT be used to evaluate individual performance. Once you have group logs for a few days, start your analysis looking at everything from a group perspective.

Time management software

Computer programs which allow you to consolidate schedules and reminders. You can also be provided with a printout of your **calendar**, your daily **'to do' list** and reminder notes. If you need memory prompts for **appointments**, you can program your software to beep reminders whenever you need them. Check these features before you purchase:

1 On-screen displays and hard copy easy to follow; laid out sensibly.
2 Easy to operate.
3 Colour-coded display of schedules: monthly, weekly and daily versions.

4 Capacity to block in schedules in different colours for different activities; useful for readily detecting conflicts.
5 Ability to key in a regular meeting once only and have it automatically added to your schedule.
6 Text search; can search out notes on specific events and display (or print) a calendar showing only those events.
7 Address storage and phone-dialling capabilities and/or interfaces to use these.

Time management software focuses on a few tasks, and it's easy to learn to use. Make certain you are going to take the time to use it, however, before you make the investment.

Time measurement

A term frequently interchanged with **work measurement**. It is sometimes used to describe the process of using a **time log**.

Time orientation

The time sense in which you give emphasis to the past, the present or the future. This can create dramatic differences in a person's sense of time urgency, focus or pace. The ideal time management perspective is a balance between present and future with past blended in.

Future-oriented people have their eye on the horizon. They enjoy setting **goals** and action steps. They are concerned about 'breaking new ground'. Once they have some specific commitments they can easily resist the temptation to play when there's work to be done, although they can lose sight of the 'how to' at times. They usually begin working on assignments early. Under pressure they tend to jump about too much raising too many issues. Future-oriented people always have a working watch, a **diary** and a **'to do' list**. They frequently talk about what they will be doing next week, next month, next year.

Present-oriented people are practical and to the point. They take a 'there and now' attitude toward life. They are interested in concrete things and tend to ignore those who talk about long-range **goals**. On the one hand they try to resolve things quickly, on the other hand they need to be very sure something will bring tangible returns before they spend time and

energy on it. They are good at handling an immediate crisis and derive satisfaction from how well they get along with their co-workers. They are often in a frenzy of activity and the current moment is the only one that is important. Waiting is painful for them. If told to be patient and to delay something a month or two, they will resort to all sorts of manoeuvres to get things moving.

Past-oriented people are more interested in preserving the accomplishments of the past than in creating something new. They are conservative and will always measure new ideas against past practices. They are empathetic and understanding and are always trying to place themselves in 'others' shoes'. You can tell past-oriented people when you hear them saying 'we've always done things that way around here'. Instead of actively refusing new ideas they will continue to 'check it' or 'give it further thought'. Past-oriented people are usually not punctual. If they own a watch they frequently forget to wear it. Their lunches take too long and they can extend a brief coffee break into a half-hour chat. They are relaxed and philosophical if kept waiting. They talk about 'living one day at a time' and 'whatever will be, will be', and do not have a sense of urgency.

What is your time orientation? What is the time orientation of your team members? There are obvious advantages and disadvantages in each orientation. It can be helpful to point out to team members your own orientation and discuss differences, strengths and weaknesses.

When building a new team, consider the mix of orientations—perhaps include some future-oriented planners, some present-oriented facilitators and a past-oriented person with an appreciation of the traditions of the organisation.

Time span measurement

The measurement of the complexity of each role or position in an employment system. According to Elliott Jaques, author of *Requisite Organization*, the longest task or program of work assigned to a manager or other employee, throughout which that individual is required to use their discretion in how to go about achieving the **goal** results by the targeted completion date, has been found to have a direct relationship to the level of complexity of their overall role.

Any two or more roles with the same time span (longest task in the role), regardless of occupation, will have the same level of complexity of information and work requirements; and, to be successfully filled, will require individuals who have essentially the same **time horizon**.

For example, a first line manager may have (as the longest task in their role) six months to carry through a training program to upgrade the effectiveness of their team. Similarly, a senior sales representative may undertake a special search for potential customers over a six-month period. Each of these roles has as its longest targeted completion time a six-month period. According to Jaques the two roles are therefore equally complex, even though the skilled use of knowledge is quite different.

Time standard

A term used in time and **work measurement** to indicate the base time allowed for a defined unit of work to be finished to a specified quality. The standard is used as a guide to the setting of work standards within organisations.

Time wasters

Things which consume time and keep you from achieving your objectives. Also known as 'time robbers'. There is no set formula for coping with time wasters as they are different for everyone. Time wasters can be internal, coming from within you; or external, caused by someone or something else. A systematic approach is required when dealing with time wasters so that you can identify the probable causes and come up with the right solutions. See the **Quick reference guide** later in this book for a list of some of the most common time wasters and where you might look for solutions.

'To do' list

A simple, prioritised list of non-recurring things to do each day which is considered an essential time management tool. A 'to do' list is also helpful in identifying things that should *not* be done.

'To do' lists on loose pieces of paper are *out*. They get lost. There is also a risk that you will throw away one which has an important phone number written on it. Use a **planner**, a **diary** (rule a line down the page and use one part for your 'to do' list) or even a special book just for that purpose. Right-brain dominant people (see **Brain dominance**) need colourful notebooks. Try fabric covers. Perhaps yellow pads in three sizes. Right-brain dominant people get bored with one simple method so they need multiple stimuli to remind them to use their list. Perhaps a different colour pad for each day of the week. You can purchase special pads of printed 'to do' lists with sections such as TO DO/TO CALL/TO WRITE. These are fine if they help you.

Follow these general guidelines for preparing and using your 'to do' list:

1 Make preparing your list a habit. Do it at the same time— the first or last quarter hour of each day, or both—and in the same place.
2 Add items to your list from your **master list**, from diary notes, from your **follow-up system**. Also add items as you work through your in-tray (phone messages, faxes, memos).
3 As you list each item ask, 'Why me?'. Delegate wherever possible.
4 The size of the list is not important but don't go overboard. Too many items will mean that your list will be come a **visual stressor**.
5 Prioritise your list, ranking items in terms of payoff:
   A – high payoff – definitely must do
   B – negative payoff – high risk if not done
   C – medium payoff – basics
   D – low or non-existent payoff
6 **Consolidate** your list, **grouping** or batching like tasks.
7 Transfer your top five **priorities** to your **calendar**. Block in **appointments** with yourself to work on these tasks. As you do this, consider the practical factor (hours, time of day,

people involved), the biological factor (**prime time**, **energy** levels) and the deadline factor (how urgent).

8 Review your list. If the same item keeps appearing on several 'to do' lists do it, **delegate** it or drop it.
9 Use today's 'to do' list as the starting point for tomorrow's list.
10 Remember to do a little **elephant eating** each day.

Your 'to do' list can also become a simple device to help you monitor your time and to develop some norms for tasks done regularly. Annotate your list with notes showing how the hours went. Then assemble a week's worth of lists and look for patterns. Ask yourself these questions:

1 Why didn't I do all the items?
2 Did the priorities of other people take precedence over my own?
3 Did I have enough time for minor but essential tasks?
4 Did I have time for the unexpected?
5 What were the **time wasters**?
6 Does my list match my job description?

Toe first principle

One approach to starting a task. Think of taking a swim in the ocean. Some people start by putting their toe in first and then gradually enter the water, letting their body adjust to the temperature. Others run quickly across the sand and dive straight in.

The 'toe first' principle has some merit in beginning a task. It gives you time to think about your problem, determining which is the best course of action. However, while you are thinking about whether to 'get wet' or not the clock is ticking over. When too much time has elapsed, you are into the 'paralysis by analysis' syndrome. On the other hand, if you 'jump first, think later' you make a good head start but can get caught later because of your lack of **planning**.

Neither approach is ideal, but most of us have a preference for one or the other. Try different approaches until you find the rhythm that best equates with your most effective way of working.

Tools

Anything you use to help achieve your time management goals. It is important to have the right tools for the right job. Pencils, paper, calculators; desks, chairs, tables; computers, photocopiers, fax machines. Some 'tools' are less obvious, e.g. your car, your newspaper, a foreign language you speak, your accounting qualification.

Travel time

Something business people engage in a great deal without asking whether it is really necessary. Ask yourself these questions to help evaluate your travel time:

1 Should someone else be making this trip—not only to save my time but also for that person's development?
2 Will making the trip have a constructive bearing on the results I am seeking?
3 Does obtaining the results require personal contact? If not, how else can I obtain them?
4 Will the contacts be useful for future information sources, aside from the specific objective of the trip?
5 How long since I have visited the person or location? Is the frequency of the trip necessary? What would happen if I visited the person or location less often?
6 How much will the trip cost in salary and expenses? Is the cost justified?

If you travel frequently, you can save time by building up a 'travel collection' that is ready to go whenever you are. Start by setting up a travel **briefcase** which contains your 'portable office'. You can purchase readymade sets of office requisites which consist of miniature stapler, tape holder, hole punch, ruler, scissors, etc. or you can make up your own set. Also keep a folder of letterheads, envelopes (stamped if possible) and other business forms, a collection of **business cards**, a minirecorder, an envelope for storing all your travel receipts, and a spare set of important **telephone** numbers. If your trip requires several stopovers, organise the sections in your briefcase accordingly. Laptop computers are great time savers.

Have standard items such as toiletries and cosmetics pre-packed and have a pre-packed overnight kit. In your kit include an extra pair of glasses and any medication you require. Replenish your stock *at the end of each trip* so that you can be ready to go at short notice.

Develop *three* personal 'take with you' lists: one for overnight, one for a week in one place, and one for a trip with two to three stopovers. If you are a 'sole' parent, assemble a 'While I'm Away' notebook with advice about what to do if the children or the dog gets sick, if the washing machine breaks down, and so on. Remember to leave a spare copy of your **itinerary** for home use.

Travel light. Stick to one basic colour pattern and coordinate shoes and accessories. Buy wrinkle-free clothing. Travelling in business clothes means one less outfit to pack. Select travel luggage carefully. Consider having three different cases: an overnight, a two–three night (both of 'carry on' size) and a one-week plus. To protect your back, select cases with inbuilt wheels or purchase a durable set of luggage wheels. Identify your luggage inside as well as out (include a phone number) in case the luggage is lost and the tag is missing. Pack systematically. Lay everything out on the bed and pack in order. Consider packing some clothing in large plastic bags to separate different types of garments.

Have four copies of your itinerary: one in your briefcase, one in your pocket or purse, one in the office, and one at home. A good itinerary lists telephone numbers, addresses, hire car arrangements, **appointment** times, etc. Commuting time between appointments needs to be considered. Do not overschedule, and confirm all appointments before departure. It is also advisable to have an alternative plan just in case.

Read briefing papers or material *before* you leave; research indicates that information is not absorbed and retained as well when you are travelling. If you fly you can always re-read en route.

Avoid the herd instinct and fly outside 'peak hours'. Also, consider traffic when driving—appointments between 10 am and 2 pm save considerable driving time.

If you fly:

1 Don't underestimate a good travel agent.
2 Join a flight club and use the facilities—fax, phone, photocopier, computers, meeting space.

3 Decide your preference for aircraft seating. Some people prefer window seats because you have fewer interruptions. Others prefer the aisle for more leg room and a faster exit.

4 Rest before you travel and limit alcohol, tea and coffee consumption.

5 Consider flying the night before your meeting.

6 During the flight you can work on a long-term project you have been avoiding, rehearse speeches, presentations and interviews, listen to tapes, catch up on professional **reading** (not the airline's magazines), dictate correspondence, write on your laptop computer.

7 Remember to exercise during a long flight. Get out of your seat once an hour and walk up and down the aisle; while seated, flex your feet and rotate your ankles; simulate walking by sitting up straight, lifting your knees slightly and shifting your weight from leg to leg; stretch your neck and shoulders by turning your head and stretching your arms above your head.

8 Drink lots of water and avoid alcohol which can dehydrate you and make you drowsy.

If you drive:

1 Ask for a parking spot when making your appointments.

2 Take a **mobile phone**.

3 Arrange to have multiple appointments in the same general location.

4 Listen to tapes while driving.

5 Dictate while driving.

On overnight stopovers, learn to say '**no**' to peer pressure and to travel companions who want to play cards or have a night on the town.

Plan your return for the end of the day so that you can go home and rest—or for the start of a normal day so that you can go directly to work (see **Re-entry**). Never assume anything and plan for the unexpected! There is rarely such a thing as hassle-free travel.

Triage

A system used in times of war to sort casualties into categories of priority for treatment. Triage is used when medical aid and materials are in short supply and doctors have to decide who to treat. This is a useful model for setting work **priorities**. The categories are:

1 Victim will likely die, don't treat.
2 Is injured but can wait for treatment.
3 Needs immediate attention or operation.

Type A behaviour

A coronary-prone behaviour pattern. As a result of a study of 3000 healthy middle-aged men conducted in the 1960s, the researching physicians maintained that coronary heart disease is caused mainly by psychological rather than hereditary or dietary factors.

Type A behaviour is described by Jere Yates in *Managing Stress* as 'an action-emotion complex that can be observed in any person who is *aggressively* involved in a chronic, incessant struggle to achieve more and more in less and less time. . .' These people contrast with Type Bs who are simply non-As— people who don't so readily suffer heart attacks.

You are a typical Type A if you:

1 Tend to gesture expressively when you talk; explosively accentuate key words in ordinary speech; have difficulty controlling nervous mannerisms.
2 Always move, walk and eat rapidly.
3 Feel and openly show impatience with the rate at which most events take place.
4 Get unduly irritated at delays.
5 Often try to do two things at once.
6 Have trouble sitting around doing nothing; almost always feel vaguely guilty when you relax.
7 Find yourself scheduling more and more things in less and less time.
8 Make a fetish of being punctual.
9 Get impatient when you watch others doing things you think you can do better or faster.
10 Always play to win, even if playing a game with a child.

If you show signs of being a Type A, here are some strategies:

1 Read and follow suggestions on **stress** reduction and **relaxation**.
2 Consider revising your daily schedule to allow more time for you to be alone.
3 Seek support from Type B personalities and cultivate more Type B friendships.
4 Eliminate luncheons and other social activities at which you continue to talk and think about the same things as you do at work.
5 If you are the senior person in your team, try to let the others do most of the talking.

U

U-shape

The way paperwork should flow—from right to left—for easy control. When setting up your desk layout, the in-tray goes in the top right-hand corner, items for follow-up in a drawer on the bottom right-hand side, items for immediate attention go to the base of the 'U' where you are sitting, and completed items go to the out-tray on the top left-hand corner. If you are left-handed, the reverse of this may feel more comfortable.

Un-schedule

A weekly calendar of all your committed activities which shows how much time is available to work towards a primary goal. An un-schedule can be a useful anti-**procrastination** device.

Start with a sheet of paper ruled into columns for days of the week and rows for hours of the day. Then write in all the things you have fixed on your schedule for the next week. If you don't know exactly, make an educated guess and write it down. This is not what you would like to be doing or should be doing but what is already committed.

When your un-schedule is finished, the blanks show your uncommitted time. As you visualise yourself going through the week, if your un-schedule is very full the first reaction will be anxiety. When you get over the initial shock, see what you can learn about how you manage your time. Consider:

1 What is the extent of your 'free' time?
2 Is there sufficient time to work on your primary goals?
3 How realistic are the time commitments?
4 Do you have sufficient time alone or do you do too much socialising?

5 What have you not enough of scheduled, e.g. time with family?
6 How could you revise your schedule?

Unit managing director concept

A concept that everyone in an organisation is the managing director of that portion of the organisation over which they have control. If one of your staff is in charge of mail, get them to see themself as the Managing Director of Mail. In that role they will be encouraged to make decisions, solve their own problems and sort out conflicts. The more managing directors you have reporting to you, the fewer interruptions you are likely to have.

Urgent v. important

Urgent and important are labels often wrongly given to tasks. A task that advances a **goal** or **objective** is important; a job that has to be done immediately is urgent. The urgent task may have short-term consequences and may or may not contribute to your objectives.

The late US President, General Eisenhower, observed that there seemed to be an inverse relationship between importance and urgency; that is, the more important an item was, the less likely it was to be urgent, and vice versa.

Overconcern with the 'urgent' rather than the 'important' causes a syndrome known as the 'tyranny of the urgent'. This tyranny is the result of lack of **planning** and it creates unnecessary pressure and distorts **priorities**. Analyse your activities carefully to help distinguish the urgent from the important. Then set your plan accordingly.

V

Values

Consciously or unconsciously held beliefs, on which everything we do, every decision we make, is based. Values determine motivation and are linked with time and effort. Lack of value clarification can slow down your time management. For example, consider these aspects:

1 Acting one way in a situation and later regretting it or wishing you had behaved differently (can't say '**no**').
2 Settling for whatever comes next, rather than pursuing your own **goals** (goal setting).
3 Making a decision between two or more alternatives (**procrastination**, **decision making**, conflict resolution).
4 Ability to trust (**delegation**, team building).
5 Risk-taking capacity (**delegation**, **planning**, **productivity**).
6 Doing things out of compulsion or habit, rather than out of conscious choice (planning, goal setting).
7 Demanding perfection (general time management).
8 Left-over feelings of inadequacy or guilt (risk taking).

Videoconferencing

An alternative to face-to-face **meetings**, using public videoconferencing rooms or a dedicated facility on your own premises. It can be a very effective use of time for round table discussions, crisis meetings, research briefings and product launches. Videoconferencing is easy to schedule, reduces the need for frequent travel, can involve more people, can use guest speakers and may cost less.

Videoconferencing is an enhancement of **teleconferencing**

as it enables you to see speakers as well as hear them. The facilities are secure and include facsimile, graphics cameras, VHS recorders and whiteboards. Documents and graphics can be sent via the medium spontaneously.

Since meeting start and finish times are scheduled in advance, participants find they stick more closely to the **agenda** and accomplish their business in a shorter period. If additional time is required, however, extensions can be made with notice 15 minutes prior to the allotted finishing time.

Visual stressor

Something you can see which creates anxiety and drains your **energy**, e.g. a cluttered bulletin board, a disorganised **desk**, a full in-tray, a crowded **diary**. If you feel overloaded because of visual stressors, you are more likely to **procrastinate**. If you have started your task you can be easily distracted thus slowing down your **productivity**. Follow the 'out of sight, out of mind' rule and put visual stressors where you cannot see them.

A visual stressor can also be something related to the design and layout of your office, as for example in an open office located next to a walk-through with people constantly passing near your desk. See if you can change the angle of your desk or place some plants in such a way that they block your view. Or negotiate a change of location or layout with your manager.

Visualisation

A technique, also known as 'imaging', of using your imagination to create a mental picture in your mind. It can be used for creating ideas, visualising solutions, changing behaviour. Everyone visualises differently. Some people actually 'see' images, others 'hear' images, still others 'visualise' through their feelings.

For visualisation to be effective you must *want* to bring about change and must believe that it can happen. For a basic exercise in visualisation:

1 Write down in a short sentence or two an **affirmation** about what you want to change as a result of your imaging.

2 Sit or lie in a comfortable position in a quiet place.
3 Relax, close your eyes and breathe deeply.
4 Count backwards slowly from 10 to 1.
5 When you feel relaxed, imagine the situation happening exactly as you want it to. Imagine the atmosphere and the setting; what people are wearing, what they are saying. Even the temperature.
6 Keeping the image in mind, state your affirmation to yourself.
7 Keep repeating the affirmation, breathe deeply and stay relaxed for at least five minutes, or as long as it is enjoyable.
8 Repeat the process at least once a day.

Vocational time

The time a manager spends *doing* something rather than *getting it done through others*. All managers have to do some vocational tasks (training staff, reading professional journals, collecting **planning** data), but some do more than they should. Why? Because they enjoy it.

Volcano effect

The way in which some people keep paperwork on their desks. It is easily recognised, as it looks as though everything has been spewed out in a massive eruption. There is always a more or less clear area in the middle of the desk where the work is done—a crater in a vaguely conical heap of papers, books and files. According to volcano theory, the further something is from the crater the less immediately relevant it is. Eventually, the most useless papers become buried, move slowly down and across the desk and fall to the floor to be swept away by the cleaners. This is one method of keeping **filing** to a minimum.

W

Waiting time

Something to be given up forever. Do not see it as waiting time but rather as catch-up time. Do some **reading**, draft a memo, update your **'to do' list**.

Wake-up breaks

Short breaks taken every 15–30 minutes to re-energise yourself and help you maintain your alertness. Examples include changing your position at the desk, standing or stretching for a minute, doing a little running in place, taking a short quick walk, rinsing your face with cold water. (See also **Joy breaks**.)

Wall calendar

A large **calendar** which hangs on the wall and is useful for long-term **planning**. A typical wall calendar has large squares for each date on which you can enter such things as project schedules, rosters, vacation times or staff assignments. Use colours to help distinguish components or individuals noted on the calendar. You can purchase wall calendars which are magnetic. You can then use moveable magnetic strips (also available in colour) to identify different items.

Wants inventory

A technique which allows you to use 'don't wants' to help you uncover what you 'do want'. To prepare your wants inventory, divide a sheet of paper into two columns headed 'Want More Of' and 'Want Less Of'. Make a list in each column considering all aspects of your life: work, leisure, personal, achievements, lifestyle. Try to *balance your list* writing a 'More Of' for every 'Less Of'. Now circle the 'More Ofs' which are most important to you.

Make a new list every day for a week without referring to your previous list. Then compare the five lists. Use them as a basis for setting objectives. Repeat this technique every month to help you revise and revalue your **objectives**.

Warm-ups

A way of easing into **paperwork** if you have been away from your **desk** for a while. Just as athletes warm up before physical exercise, mental athletes need to warm up before they tackle their in-trays. To warm up, start with short memos then go on to letters. Once you are in full stride, move on to **reports** and larger documents. (See also **Re-entry**.)

Workaholic

Someone who is addicted to work. Workaholics are seen by non-workaholics as people with a social disease which has distorted their personal development. People who work to live cannot understand people who live to work and love it. Other workaholics, or aspiring workaholics, consider workaholism a virtue. Symptoms of workaholism? Do you:

1 Get up early, no matter how late you go to bed.
2 Communicate better with co-workers than with friends and family.
3 Read or work while you eat.
4 Consistently take work home on nights and weekends.
5 See your boss's face on the tennis ball.
6 Take work to bed if you are sick.
7 Resist taking vacations.
8 Find it hard to 'do nothing'.
9 Wake up at night worrying about work problems.
10 Dread retirement.
11 Find it impossible to function without a **'to do' list**.
12 Talk 'shop' on social occasions.

13 Limit outside **reading** to work-related books and periodicals.

Lest workaholics reading this feel depressed, research shows that many of them are remarkably satisfied and content with their lives. But if you are not comfortable with your life go back to basics, resetting your **objectives** and attempting to match your lifestyle accordingly. Good **stress management** techniques help.

Work measurement

A term used to describe one of the basic components of scientific management. Work measurement is used to measure **productivity** in terms of the amount of time consumed to produce a unit of output. It can help determine performance standards and create reliable schedules. Quantity, quality and descriptive standards can be established.

There are both advantages and disadvantages in work measurement. *Some advantages are:*

1 If done correctly, standards developed are very accurate.
2 Standards help increase efficiency and communicate to employees the productivity levels expected.
3 Standards assist managers in making personnel decisions.
4 If employees are aware of procedures, less supervision is needed.
5 Standards provide a basis for incentive systems.
6 Standards can help increase morale by making employees aware of what is expected of them.

Some disadvantages:

1 Employees tend to have a negative reaction to standards determined on the basis of stopwatch studies.
2 The measurement process requires the use of a trained analyst which makes it costly.
3 Many office and managerial tasks do not easily lend themselves to work measurement.

Some of the common terms associated with work measurement include *Motion–Time Analysis (MTA), Methods Time Measurement (MTM), Basic Motion–Time Study (BMT), Universal*

Maintenance Standards (UMS), and *Master Clerical Data (MCD)*. Although the same basic principles were originally used in developing each of the systems, specific details of the various systems differ significantly. (See also **Time standard; Sampling of work activity**.)

Work style

The approach you use when you tackle a task. Higher **productivity** will result if you match the style to the task. Work flows better with some tasks if you begin at the core of the task and work out towards the edges. Other tasks are better approached from the edges, working in towards the core. Some tasks go smoother if you work in longish '**blocks**' of time. Others lend themselves to 'short bursts'.

Whatever style you use, consider the deadlines and try to work to a natural stopping point. Remember to leave yourself a reminder note so that you pick up the process and your thoughts immediately you resume working on that task.

Worry list

A useful **procrastination** prevention device. Start by writing down all the things you are currently worried about. Include potential disasters and horrors—anything that you think might go wrong. Every couple of weeks read over your list to see what actually happened. Gradually you will discover that most of your fears do not materialise. This should help you to worry less.

Worst first strategy

A way to create momentum which seems to work for some people. Start the day, or a project, by tackling the most difficult or sensitive task first thing. Deal with unpleasant people and issues right off the bat. Get your most dreaded assignments out of the way, leaving your remaining **energy** for the rest of the day. Once the worst is out of the way, all that is ahead of you are the easy pleasant things and you'll get through these with ease. (See also **Procrastination.**)

Writing

Something we should do less of, while communicating more. Writing takes time, is lonely, is hard work, gives little control over the reader's response, and makes our words permanent— including the mistakes. Try phoning instead.

Respond to correspondence with marginal notes or Post-it notes. **Delegate** writing tasks. Use **electronic mail** to cut down the size of communications. If you do a good deal of writing, learn to key in on your computer at at least 50 words per minute. Write during your high **energy** time.

Writing better and faster, without anxiety, is the wish of all time managers. The most effective writing process begins quickly and ends slowly and carefully. Follow these simple guidelines:

1 Start with plenty of paper. Initially, blank paper may be better than lined as it will allow you to write more freely.
2 Write. Write to yourself. Write anything. Brainstorm ideas using **clustering** or **mind mapping**. Get the words and ideas flowing.
3 Start your rough draft. Begin anywhere other than the beginning. Write very quickly. Write to express not impress. Use a style which is natural to you. Don't underestimate your reader's intelligence or overestimate their knowledge. Don't edit.
4 Put a summary sentence at the very beginning. This tells your reader exactly what you want them to do or know. It also helps to shape and organise your document.
5 Edit your draft. Fix the simple bits first, then look at sentences that don't say what you mean. Don't strive for perfection. (See also **Report writing.**)

X

X-method

A way to make progress when stuck for a solution to a problem. Most of us expend a good deal of time trying to find *the* key to a problem. By using the X-method you don't keep looking for the solution, waiting for a brainwave. You create a solution called x and move to the next problem. This frees you from the left-brain pressure (see also **Brain dominance**) of having to find the logical solution, allowing your right brain to search subconsciously for the answer.

General MacArthur used a kind of X-method during World War II. When he couldn't conquer one South Pacific island he bypassed it to take another.

Y

'Yes' letters

A quick formula for writing and telling someone what they want to hear. It works like this:

1 Tell them the good news.
2 Explain what it means.
3 Close with a goodwill statement.

Here, on the other hand, is a quick formula for a 'No' letter:

1 Start with a neutral statement.
2 Explain why the news is bad.
3 Tell them the bad news.
4 Suggest alternatives.
5 Close with a goodwill statement.

Z

Zero-based time budgeting

A means to help you evaluate time use starting from zero. Four times a year keep a **time log**. Analyse the log and question each task. Ask yourself whether you would start doing each task now if you weren't already doing it. If the answer is 'no', stop doing it. If the answer is 'yes', allocate it a strict time quota and stick to it.

Apply a similar approach to **paperwork** management. Before you create a letter, memo or **report** ask yourself what its real value is. If the answer is 'very little', don't produce it.

Quick reference guide

Use these pages to find the As Bs or Zs that relate to the topic that you are concerned about.

Communication:
If communication time is being wasted; messages are not getting through. . .

ASAP
Authority
Back talk
Boss
Business cards
Cassette recorder
Circles
Circle overlap
Contact file
Electronic mail
Gonnas
Journal

Motivation
'No'
Perceptual conflict
Principle of calculated
   neglect
Referral slip
Resource file
Secretary's time
Shouldas
Stalling
Synergy

Controls/standards:
If time standards and deadlines are not being met; information is not being followed up. . .

Controls
Deadlines
Delegation
Filing
Follow-up system
Monochronic time
Sampling
Standard data

Stolen time
Tickler file
Time log
Time measurement
Time span measurement
Time standard
Work measurement

Crisis management:
If there is too much management by crisis. . .

Blocks
Brainstorming
Crisis management
Deadline

Efficiency v. effectiveness
Elimination principle
Note approach
Time log

Decision making:
If decisions take too long to make and are not effective. . .

Action
Blocks
Brainstorming
Decidophobia
Decision making

Fence sitter
Flowchart
Indecision
Problem solving

Delegation:
If delegated assignments are not being completed on time and to the required standard. . .

Accountability
Authority
Circle overlap
Cliff hangers
Delegation
Freedom trail
Gonnas
Hierarchy of wasted effort
Management by exception
Monkey

Principle of calculated
  neglect
Responsibility
Responsibility chart
Reverse delegation
Shouldas
Subordinate tyranny
Synergy
Talent–time assessment
Unit managing director
  concept

Desk management:
If your desk is messy and it takes too long to find what you want. . .

C-drawer
Desk workbook
Everything out
G.U.T.S.
Parking system

Right angler
Stacked desk syndrome
U-shape
Volcano effect

Drop-in visitors:
If drop-in visitors are causing too many interruptions. . .

Availability hours
D & I chart
Drop-in visitors
Green light time
Interruptions

Open-door policy
Quiet time
Red light time
Siberia sendoff
Time Log

Efficiency v effectiveness:
If you seem to be working hard but not producing much. . .

Activity trap
Alternative principle
ASAP
'Buckets of sweat' syndrome
Doubling up

Efficiency v. effectiveness
Low payoff activities
Quickie
Rabbit chasers
Urgent v. important

Goal setting:
If productivity is low and results are not what you would like them to be. . .

Brain dominance
Eighty–twenty rule
Elephant eating
Goals
Goal calendar
Low payoff activities

Key results areas
Limited targeting
Mission statement
Targeting
Time horizon

Home organisation:
If your household management is not as you would like it to be. . .

Bartering
Bill paying
Children
Dual career couples
Financial master list
Homework habit

Household time
  management
Kitchen message centre
Leisure time
Progressive dressing
Superwoman

Ideas/creativity:
If you can't find thinking time and good ideas aren't there when you need them. . .

Backing off

Brain dominance

Brainstorming

Green light time

Clustering

Ideas notebook

Master list

Mind mapping

Navy pretest

Perhaps list

Prime time

Problem solving

X-method

Interruptions:
If you are constantly interrupted. . .

Availability hours

D & I chart

Drop-in visitors

Green light time

Quiet time

Red light time

Telephone

Time log

Meetings:
If there are too many meetings, they are taking too long, and few valuable decisions are being made. . .

Agenda

Committees

Critique

Meetings

Meetings scorecard

Teleconferencing

Videoconferencing

Paperwork:
If paperwork is excessive and you can't get it under control. . .

Bill paying

C-drawer

Categories

Charge-out system

Chrono file

Colour coding

Cross referencing

Desk workbook

File spread

Filing

Follow-up systems

Index cards

Measles method

Paperwork

Progressive filing

Reports

Tear system

Tickler file

Personal organisation:
If you seem to be tackling too many jobs at once and spend too much time on minor jobs. . .

Briefcase
Checklists
Colour coding
Consolidation
Crisis management
Discretionary time
Grouping
Homework habit
On-time personality
Sprinting concept
Time management software
Vocational time

Physical work environment:
If your work environment is not comfortable and seems to be slowing you down. . .

Accessories
Desk
Environment
Equipment overload
Ergonomics
Proxemics
Tools
Visual stressor

Planning:
If you underestimate how long things will take and are not meeting objectives. . .

Appointments
Backwards planning
Bio-rhythms
Blocking in
Charts
Deadline
Diary
Lists
'Not to do' list
Planner
Planning
Priorities
Pricing your time
Secretary's time
Start time
Time budget
Time log
Time management software
'To do' list
Triage
Un-schedule
Wall calendar
Zero-based time budgeting

Procrastination:
If you take a long time to get started on tasks and keep putting things off. . .

Affirmations
Backing off
Behaviour change
Brain dominance
Buy-in
Deadline
Discomfort dodging
Energy
Fear of failure
Habit

'No'
Pathfinders
Procrastination
Toe first principle

Visualisation
Wants inventory
Worry list
Worst first strategy

Reading/writing/presenting:
If it takes you a long time to write a letter, report or presentation; if you are behind in your professional reading. . .

ASAP
Cassette recorder
Clustering
Cooperative reading
Dictation
Electronic mail
Index cards
Information search
Mail
Mind mapping

Paragraph book
Presentation
Reference material
Reports
Simplified letter
Speed writing
Star diagram
Waiting time
Writing
'Yes' letters

Scheduling:
If schedules are not being met, set or followed. . .

Appointments
Blocking in
Charts
Checklists
Deadline
Diary
Eighty–twenty rule
Gantt charts
Flowchart
Grouping

Prime time
Project management
'To do' list
Vocational time
Scheduling
Time measurement
Time standard
Un-schedule
Work measurement

Stress/burnout:
If you work too long without a break, are feeling tired and run down, and your productivity is decreasing. . .

Addictivities
Adrenalin addiction
Affirmations
Bio-rhythms
Burnout

Chronobiology
Energy
Joy break
Journal
Leisure time

Pace of life
Preferred day assessment
Prime time
Relaxation
Stress

Type A behaviour
Visualisation
Wake-up breaks
Workaholic

Telephone:
If telephone calls are taking more time to make and receive than you think they should, and you are getting too many calls. . .

Answering machine
D & I chart
Hook
Interruptions
Quiet time

Teleconferencing
Telephone
Telephone hour
Telephone tag
Time log

Travel:
If you seem to be travelling too much for little return and have too much waiting time. . .

Cassette recorder
Checklists
Cultural time
Commuting time
Itinerary
Progressive dressing

Re-entry
Sales time
Telecommuting
Teleconferencing
Videoconferencing

Bibliography

Agor, Weston H. 1984, *Intuitive Management*, Prentice Hall, Englewood Cliffs

Albrecht, Karl 1979, *Stress and the Manager*, Prentice Hall, Englewood Cliffs

Allen, Jane E. 1986, *Beyond Time Management*, Addison-Wesley, Reading

Argyris, Chris 1964, *Integrating the Industrial and the Organization*, John Wiley & Sons, New York

Baker, Stephen 1984, *I Hate Meetings*, Collins, Sydney

Benson, Herbert 1975, *The Relaxation Response*, William Morrow & Company, New York

Bittel, Lester R. 1991, *Right on Time*, McGraw-Hill, New York

Blake, R. R. and Mouton, J. S. 1978, *Making Experience Work*, McGraw-Hill, New York

Bliss, Edwin C. 1984, *Doing It Now*, Bantam, New York

Booth, Audrey L. 1988, *Less Stress, More Success*, Severn House, London

Braiker, Harriet B. 1987, *The E-Type Woman*, Angus & Robertson, North Ryde

Brooks, William T. and Mullins, Terry W. 1989, *High Impact Time Management*, Prentice Hall, New Jersey

Burka, Jane B. and Yuen, Lenora M. 1983, *Procrastination*, Addison-Wesley, Reading

Cacioppe, Ron 1989, *Mind Maps*, Integra, Perth

Cannie, Joan K. 1980, *Take Charge*, Prentice Hall, Englewood Cliffs

Charlesworth, Edward A. & Nathan, Ronald 1984, *Stress Management*, Atheneum, New York

Conran, Shirley & Sidney, Elizabeth 1979, *FutureWoman*, Penguin, Melbourne

Covey, Stephen R. 1989, *The 7 Habits of Highly Effective People*, Fireside, New York

Deep, Sam & Sussman, Lyle 1990, *Smart Moves*, Addison-Wesley, Reading

DiAntonio, Steve 1986, *Making Time*, Ballantine Books, New York

Douglass, Merrill E. & Douglass, Donna A. 1980, *Manage Your Time, Manage Your Work, Manage Yourself*, AMACOM, New York

Douglass, Merrill E. and Goodwin, Phillip H. 1980, *Successful Time Management for Hospital Administrators*, AMACOM, New York

Eisenberg, Ronni and Kelly, Kate 1986, *Organise Yourself*, Piatkus, London

Ellis, Darryl J. and Pekar, Peter P. 1980, *Planning for Non-Planners*, AMACON, New York

Ferner, Jack D. 1980, *Successful Time Management*, John Wiley, New York

Freudenberger, Herbert J. 1980, *Burn Out*, Bantam Books, New York

Gawain, Shakti 1985, *Creative Visualization*, Bantam Books, New York

Goldfein, Donna 1977, *Every Woman's Guide to Time Management*, Les Feemes, Millbrae

Goodloe, A. Bensahel, J. and Kelly, J. 1984, *Managing Yourself*, Franklin Watts, New York

Greenberg, Herbert M. 1980, *Coping with Job Stress*, Prentice Hall, Englewood Cliffs

Greiff, Barne S. and Preston, K. Munter, 1981, *Tradeoffs*, Signet, New York

Grossman, Lee 1976, *Fat Paper*, McGraw-Hill, New York

Hermann, Ned 1990, *The Creative Brain*, Brain Books, Lake Lure

Hertzberg, Frederick, Bernard Mausner and Barbara Bloch Synyderman, 1959, *The Motivation to Work*, John Wiley & Sons, New York

Hirsch, Gretchen 1983, *Womanhours*, St Martin's Press, New York

Hunt, Diana and Hait, Pam 1990, *The Tao of Time*, Simon & Schuster, New York

Ivancevich, John M. and Ganster, Daniel C. 1987, *Job Stress*, The Haworth Press, New York

Jaffee, Dennis J. and Scott, Cynthia, 1984, *Self Renewal*, Fireside, New York

Januz, Lauren R. and Jones, Susan K. *Time Management for Executives*, Charles Scribner's Sons, New York

Jaques, Elliott 1989, *Requisite Organization*, Cason Hall, Arlington

Jenks, James M. and Kelly, John M. 1985, *Don't Do. Delegate!*, Franklin Watts, New York

Knaus, William J. 1979, *Do It Now*, Prentice Hall, Englewood Cliffs

Lakein, Alan 1973, *How to Get Control of Your Time and Your Life*, Signet Books, New York

LeBoeuf, Michael 1982, *The Productivity Challenge*, McGraw-Hill, New York

——1979, *Working Smart*, Warner Books, New York

Lebov, Myrna 1980, *Practical Tools and Techniques for Managing Time*, Executive Enterprises, New York

Levine, Robert 1989, 'The Pace of Life', *Psychology Today*, October, p. 42

Love, Sydney F. 1981, *Mastery and Management of Time*, Prentice Hall, Englewood Cliffs

Livingstone Booth, Audrey 1988, *Less Stress, More Success*, Severn House Publishers, London

Maslow, A.H. 1954, *Motivation and Personality*, Harper & Row, New York

McCormack, Mark H. 1989, 'Success Secrets, *Entrepreneur*, November, p. 18

McCay, James T. 1981, *The Management of Time*, 10th edn, Prentice Hall, Englewood Cliffs

McConkey, Dale D. 1986, *No-Nonsense Delegation*, AMACON, New York

McCullough, Bonnie 1986, *Totally Organized*, St Martin's Press, New York

McGee-Cooper, Ann 1983, *Time Management for Unmanageable People*, McGee-Cooper Associates, Dallas

——1990, *You Don't Have to Go Home from Work Exhausted!*, Bowen & Rogers, Dallas

Machlowitz, Marilyn 1980, *Workaholics*, Addison-Wesley, Reading

Mackay, Harvey, 1988, *Swim with the Sharks Without Being Eaten Alive*, Sphere Books, London

McGregor, Douglas 1960, *The Human Side of Enterprise*, McGraw-Hill Book Company, New York

McKenzie, R. Alec. 1975, *The Time Trap*, McGraw-Hill, New York

Mackoff, Barbara 1984, *Leaving the Office Behind*, General Publishing Company, Toronto

McLean, Alan A. 1986, *High Tech Survival Kit*, John Wiley & Sons, New York

Marvin, Philip 1980, *Executive Time Management*, AMACOM, New York

Materka, Pat Roessle 1982, *Time In, Time Out, Time Enough*, Prentice Hall, Englewood Cliffs

Merrill, Roger 1990, *Connections: Quadrant II Time Management*, Institute for Principle-Centered Leadership, Salt Lake City

Moskowitz, Robert 1981, *How to Organise Your Work and Your Life*, Doubleday, New Jersey

Nelson, Robert B. 1988, *Delegation*, Scott Foreman & Company, Glenview

Nichols, Carol and Lurie, Jan 1981, *Checklists*, Simon & Schuster, New York

Noon, James 1985, *A-Time*, Van Nostrand Reinhold, Wokingham

Olson, Val 1984, *White Collar Waste*, Prentice Hall, Englewood Cliffs

Oncken, William, Jr. and Donald L. Wass 1974 'Management Time: Who's got the monkey?', *Harvard Business Review*, November–December, p. 75

Oncken, William J. Jr. 1984, *Managing Management Time*, Prentice Hall, Englewood Cliffs

Ornish, Dean 1982, *Stress, Diet & Your Heart*, Holt, Rinehart & Winston, New York

Pines, A. M., Aronson, E. and Kafry, D. 1981, *Burnout*, The Free Press, New York

Prince, Ray 1984, *620,000 is All You've Got!*, Boolarong Publications, Brisbane

Rafferty, Robert 1982, *101 Lists*, World Almanac Publications, New York

Reynolds, Helen and Tramel, Mary E. 1979, *Executive Time Management*, Prentice Hall, Englewood Cliffs

Rico, Gabriele L. 1983, *Writing the Natural Way*, J. P. Tarcher, Los Angeles

Sanderson, Michael 1981, *What's the Problem Here?*, Executive Enterprises Publications, New York

Schlenger, Sunny and Roesch, Roberta 1989, *How to Be Organized in Spite of Yourself*, New American Library, New York

Scott, Dru 1980, *How to Put More Time in Your Life*, Signet, New York

Shaevitz, Marjorie Hansen 1984, *The Superwoman Syndrome*, Warner Books, New York

Shaevitz, Marjorie Hansen and Shaevitz, Morton H. 1980, *Making It Together as a Two-Career Couple*, Houghton Mifflin, Boston

Sheehy, Gail 1982, *Pathfinders*, Bantam Books, New York

Sher, Barbara 1979, *Wishcraft*, Ballantine Books, New York

Silver, Susan 1989, *Organised to be the Best*, Adams-Hall Publishing, Los Angeles

Slevin, Dennis P. and Pinto, Jeffry K. 1987, 'Balancing Strategy and Tactics in Project Implementation, *Sloan Management Review*, Fall, Volume 29, No. 1, p. 33

Steinmetz, J. Blankenship, J. et al., 1980, *Managing Stress Before It Manages You*, Bull Publishing, Palo Alto

Storz, Moni Lai 1989, *Mind–Body Power*, Time Books International, Singapore

Tarkenton, F. and Boyett, J. H. 1989, 'The Competitive Edge', *Entrepreneur*, June, p. 14

Taylor, Harold L. 1981, *Making Time Work for You*, Dell Publishing, New York

Tec, Leon 1980, *Targets*, Signet, New York

Tennov, Dorothy 1977, *Super Self*, Funk & Wagnalls, New York

Time Manager International 1986, *Key Areas*, Denmark

Turla, Peter and Hawkins, Kathleen L. 1983, *Time Management Made Easy*, E. P. Dutton, New York

Winston, Stephanie 1978, *Getting Organized*, Warner Books, New York

——1983, *The Organized Executive*, W.W. Norton, New York

Witkin-Lanoil, Georgia 1985, *The Female Stress Syndrome*, Berkley Books, New York

Yates, Jere E. 1979, *Managing Stress*, AMACOM, New York

Author's note

I want to hear *your* ideas, tips and hints. Please write to me, or send me a fax. I hope to be able to include them in future editions (with acknowledgments). Contact me care of:

Centrebrain
PO Box 46
Caulfield East, Victoria 3145
Fax: (03) 885 2652